Clay Jar, CRACKED

Clay Jar, CRACKED

WHEN WE'RE BROKEN
BUT NOT SHATTERED

CORTNEY DONELSON

New York

Clay Jar, CRACKED
WHEN WE'RE BROKEN BUT NOT SHATTERED

Published in New York, New York, by Morgan James Publishing. Morgan James and The Entrepreneurial Publisher are trademarks of Morgan James, LLC. www.MorganJamesPublishing.com

The Morgan James Speakers Group can bring authors to your live event. For more information or to book an event visit The Morgan James Speakers Group at www.TheMorganJamesSpeakersGroup.com.

Shelfie

A **free** eBook edition is available with the purchase of this print book.

CLEARLY PRINT YOUR NAME ABOVE IN UPPER CASE

Instructions to claim your free eBook edition:
1. Download the Shelfie app for Android or iOS
2. Write your name in **UPPER CASE** above
3. Use the Shelfie app to submit a photo
4. Download your eBook to any device

ISBN 978-1-68350-085-8 paperback
ISBN 978-1-68350-086-5 eBook
ISBN 978-1-68350-087-2 hardcover
Library of Congress Control Number:
2016907885

Cover Design by:
Rachel Lopez
www.r2cdesign.com

Interior Design by:
Bonnie Bushman
The Whole Caboodle Graphic Design

In an effort to support local communities, raise awareness and funds, Morgan James Publishing donates a percentage of all book sales for the life of each book to Habitat for Humanity Peninsula and Greater Williamsburg.

Get involved today! Visit
www.MorganJamesBuilds.com

DEDICATION

I dedicate this book to God and to all who seek Him, particularly those who may benefit from knowing they are not alone as they face personal challenges with faith. God made my story possible, and I thank Him and give Him all the glory for holding me together as I lived it out. He faithfully continues to make all things good.

Secondly, I dedicate this book to my husband, who supported me as I wrote it, even as it exposed private parts of our life together. It is difficult to be open about such things, but the process was healing, enlightening and filled with joy, as I believe it brought us closer to our Heavenly Father and each other.

CONTENTS

ACKNOWLEDGEMENTS

To Marc, my best friend and life partner: I love you.

To my children, I hope I have modeled that which I have taught you. Be a leader for what is right and not a follower of this world. Mom loves you.

To my dear friends, Dana, Jessica, and Tanya. You are my iron. I hope to sharpen you as much as you have me.

To the ladies of "Oaks," I will never forget my season with you. Thank you for being lights in my darkness.

To my first editor, Amy with Amy French Ink, you are a wonderful coach and encourager while being true to your craft and expertise. Thank you.

And, to Jesus, You are my everything.

INTRODUCTION

We all have a story. This is mine. It is not an easy story to share, but it is worth telling. I captured part of my story as a collection of my devotions, written over the course of my devastating experiences. My prayer is that the hybrid nature of this book—part autobiography, part devotional—does the story justice and glorifies God appropriately. I inserted the devotions throughout the story to help provide a clear picture of the wrestling happening in my heart, mind, and soul. These devotions are set apart from the story with bold lines and start with their own titles and the dates they were originally written.

On a quick read, this book might seem to be about marriage, betrayal and forgiveness. Those topics are certainly part of the story. But for me, and what I hope to express is that this book is about the power of prayer, digging into the Bible, and listening to God—no matter what. At a time when I felt weak, hopeless, and alone, connecting with a piece of Scripture strengthened my faith, saved my family, and led me to a sense of purpose and community that I deeply needed.

The Scripture I used to tell my story is 2 Corinthians 4. I wrestled with these verses for many years. Through two decades of reading the Bible, whenever I came to this passage during my quiet times, I felt something stir deep in my heart. I knew it was an important piece of God's Word for me. As I read, I felt it pulling me in and begging me to sit with it and stay awhile. Yet for a long time, I had no idea how to interpret it.

Then in my thirty's, when it seemed my world had come crashing down, 2 Corinthians 4 became the seal of my purpose. This Scripture that had beckoned me and confused me all at the same time suddenly turned into the foundational life verse from which I could live out God's will for me.

2 Corinthians 4 (NIV)

"Therefore, since through God's mercy we have this ministry, we do not lose heart. Rather, we have renounced secret and shameful ways; we do not use deception, nor do we distort the word of God. On the contrary, by setting forth the truth plainly we commend ourselves to everyone's conscience in the sight of God. And even if our gospel is veiled, it is veiled to those who are perishing. The god of this age has blinded the minds of unbelievers, so that they cannot see the light of the gospel that displays the glory of Christ, who is the image of God. For what we preach is not ourselves, but Jesus Christ as Lord, and ourselves as your servants for Jesus' sake. For God, who said, 'Let light shine out of darkness,' made his light shine in our hearts to give us the light of the knowledge of God's glory displayed in the face of Christ.

"But we have this treasure in jars of clay to show that this all-surpassing power is from God and not from us. We are hard pressed on every side, but not crushed; perplexed, but not in despair; persecuted, but not abandoned; struck down, but not destroyed. We always carry around in our body the death of Jesus, so that the life of Jesus may also be revealed in our body. For we who are alive are always being given over to death for Jesus' sake, so that his life may also be revealed in our mortal body. So then, death is at work in us, but life is at work in you.

"It is written: 'I believed; therefore I have spoken.' Since we have that same spirit of faith, we also believe and therefore speak, because we know that the one who raised the Lord Jesus from the dead will also raise us with Jesus and present us with you to himself. All this is for your benefit, so that the grace that is reaching more and more people may cause thanksgiving to overflow to the glory of God.

"Therefore we do not lose heart. Though outwardly we are wasting away, yet inwardly we are being renewed day by day. For our light and momentary troubles are achieving for us an eternal glory that far outweighs them all. So we fix our eyes not on what is seen, but on what is unseen, since what is seen is temporary, but what is unseen is eternal."

We are all fragile. On our own, we have the capacity to shatter under the pressure of this world's struggles and heartaches. But with God, we don't shatter. The Lord keeps us whole and filled with purpose if we let Him, if only we follow Him.

This is not just another book about marriage or even surviving betrayal. Nor is it primarily about learning to forgive what initially seems unforgivable. This book is about knowing God—not so much about His promises to us (there are so many and He is so faithful)—but about our assurances to Him and how we follow through on them during the ups and downs of our life stories.

When we are baptized into our positions as daughters and sons of the Almighty God, we are making Him a promise. We pledge to follow our Lord to the best of our ability—to obey Him no matter the cost. The moment we invite the Holy Spirit to enter our hearts and allow Him to pair with our souls, we have the choice to put aside all of our personal agendas, selfish ambitions, and covetous pride to truly trust and let Him lead us. We stop asking, "Why?" This book is about my struggle to keep that promise during one of the hardest times of my life, and about the blessings that came from staying true to my faith and following Jesus.

In this, my most treasured Bible verse, God prompted the disciple Paul to describe us as fragile jars made of clay. As a believer, I love God without boundaries and try to live accordingly. But neither I nor my life's circumstances are perfect, and my most difficult trials have left cracks, much like those found on used and abandoned clay jars. Yet, each crack has led me to examine how I live my faith, to identify my weak spots, to grow stronger through Christ, and to let His work in me shine through for others to witness.

The cracks remain after the hard times pass. These reminders of my imperfection are also wonderful reminders of God's perfection—because they offer more ways to let His light shine out through me, for others who seek Him to see. These cracks paint a life of intersecting lessons, healing moments, and growth. In other words, my cracks give me a beautiful story to tell.

My prayer is that this story helps someone else to appreciate his or her own cracks and fragility. I hope you finish the book with the knowledge that no matter what life hurls at you, if you keep the Lord at the forefront of your every action and thought, you will not be ruined. You will be kept whole by the Most Holy. And, when you reach the other side of your preciously horrific experience, you, too, will be able to share with others what the Lord can do if we keep our promises and follow Him.

Chapter 1
STRUCK DOWN

"But we have this treasure in jars of clay to show that this all-surpassing power is from God and not from us. We are hard pressed on every side, but not crushed; perplexed, but not in despair; persecuted, but not abandoned; struck down, but not destroyed."

—2 Corinthians 4:7–9

The scream that escaped through my pillow-covered mouth was guttural. I was on my knees with my face planted in a sofa cushion as I felt my heart and soul crack.

"We had sex."

My husband's words had struck me down. They had rendered me unable to see. I could only feel. I felt so many things all at once: anguish, disbelief, despair, lost, violated, torn apart. I screamed again after my lungs ran out of air. It was all I could do, a moaning and gnashing-of-teeth kind of scream. In just one instant, the life I thought I was leading, the family I thought we had built, and the marriage I had cherished were desecrated.

Somehow, amid swirling emotions and hazy thoughts, I remembered I had a two-year-old playing in the next room. I left my husband sitting on the floor. I walked to the kitchen and picked up my phone.

"Can you come get my daughter?" My voice was hollow, much like my heart felt. My friend stopped what she was doing and came within minutes. She whisked away my little girl to a calmer place for the moment.

As soon as the front door closed, I went to the iPad sitting on the kitchen counter and searched the Internet for a home phone number. I dialed. I had to do something. I had to take control of something.

"This is Marc's wife. I am leaving a message for John (*name changed*). As the husband of Mary (*name changed*), you should know that your wife and my husband were having an affair that included sex. I wanted you to know. Do not call me back."

I hung up. I didn't stop to assess whether that call had helped me feel better. I didn't contemplate whether it had been the right thing to do. I just knew I felt utterly blindsided, and I wanted someone else to feel that way too.

Marc had left the living room. I ran up the stairs, taking them two at a time. My heart was racing. I felt a crack widen somewhere deep in my soul. At this point, there were no tears— they would come later.

I stopped at my bedroom door. My husband was sitting on the small couch at the foot of our bed, his head in his hands. I ripped off my wedding rings and hurled them across the room at him. Next I stormed over to our wedding photo, hanging on the wall, and tore that down. We had been married thirteen years. Those years felt like a lie.

"Call her and tell her to quit." I spewed the words, giving Marc no opportunity to doubt the seriousness of my command. This was no request. There would be no debate. "If she doesn't quit then you will be the one to have to find another job."

I stood in the hallway as he tapped out numbers on his phone. My rage was building. I could feel my body start to shake; my breaths became shallow. These sensations were welcomed ones. Anger is so much easier to feel than raw heart pain. Hatred comes more smoothly than loss and anguish; it temporarily filled me with a sense of power, and I needed to believe I had some power left. I sure didn't feel I had any.

As I stood just outside my bedroom, I heard my husband on the phone. "My wife knows." There was a pause. "She knows … she knows, and you have to quit." I stepped into the room. The woman's laughter seemed to climb through the phone, and it strangled my heart. My husband's coworker informed him that she would not be leaving her job and hung up.

I hated her. And I hated the feeling of hatred, As a Christian, I believed in love and forgiveness. By the end of this story, there would be many more people I would need to stop despising and start forgiving. But in those early moments, I let anger fuel me. I returned to the hallway and paced, fists clenched. *What in this world am I supposed to do now?*

I moved back into the bedroom. I couldn't even look at Marc. "Get out. Go somewhere else and don't come back until dinner." A measure of rational thinking had returned for a moment and reminded me that our two young kids would be wondering where their dad was at dinnertime. I wasn't ready to explain his absence, so I ordered him to show back up for them, not for me.

Marc stood and moved toward the stairs. I followed him down to the door leading to the garage. He grabbed his keys, opened the door, and left without a word. As his car pulled away and the garage door rattled closed, I fell to my knees. I felt numb. My body wouldn't move. My brain seemed paralyzed as well. I couldn't think about what that evening would hold or what the next day or week might bring—nor did I much care. I would live my life in short increments in order to simply function. *Just hold on one more hour ...*

An hour did go by, and I knew I needed to get my daughter from my friend's house. I walked down the street and tried to figure out how to put words to what had happened. I already felt stunned and violated. There was no way I was ready to share details. I sat on my friend's staircase and told her Marc had admitted to having an affair. Her face communicated her pain on my behalf. Words were few. I wanted to be alone. I picked up my little girl and went back home.

Chapter 2
ABANDONED

After returning home with my daughter, I went on autopilot. I picked up my seven-year-old son from school. It was a twenty-five-minute drive to get there. My daughter napped peacefully in her car seat, and I welcomed the long silence. I drove along the interstate without thinking about the road or the other cars around me. I felt heavy in my seat, the weight of Marc's admission pressing me down, his words echoing in my mind.

Once at the school, I snapped out of my daze. My son climbed into the car, and I made a the quick and necessary decision to direct my focus on my children for the time being. I could not grasp what had happened yet. I certainly did not want them to know.

Sticking with my routine, I made dinner. My movements felt mechanical, as if my body and mind were separated. As I opened the refrigerator, I remember, I had no desire to eat and pondered how long that would last. I set the table for four, just like every other day. I wondered, *Will Marc even come home?*

Other questions loomed. *How did this happen? Do I still love him? What is unconditional love? What is going to happen next?* I couldn't reflect on them for more than a few seconds at a time; it was too painful. Again, I told myself, *Get through the next hour.*

Four hours after I had demanded he leave, Marc pulled his car into the garage. I was putting dinner on the table. My son chatted away about school and other things while he ate. He is our storyteller. My daughter listened to his tales of first grade as she picked through her dinner. As usual, her goal was simply to move the food around the plate enough to warrant a request for dessert. They sensed nothing out of the ordinary.

I stared at my food. Marc stared at me. I felt it. I couldn't look at him. If I did, all of the emotion I was holding back might break free. I feared the words that would escape my mouth and be heard by my children. I knew they would be words I could never take back. I feared damage that could not be repaired. I feared collapsing and not being able to get up. So I marched on through the evening, much like a robot. *Do the dishes. Do the bedtime routine. Get through the next hour.*

As I kissed my children good night, I wondered if we would have a truly good night anytime soon. With each of their doors closed, I let out an exhausted sigh, at last allowing myself to begin to process some of the anguish that had been building.

Standing in the dark upstairs hallway, my knees became weak. I suddenly felt very alone—*abandoned.* As I named the feeling that had been clawing at my heart all day, I recognized its uncomfortable familiarity. I thought about past hurts—hurts from my childhood and from earlier in my marriage. I thought about how I had handled them, how they had affected me, and how they had brought me to this moment.

As I slowly made my way down the steps to the family room, a dark question invaded my mind. *Would I marry this man again, now knowing the heartbreak I would endure?* We typically do not get to choose our painful stories. They just happen. This one happened so suddenly. I wondered: *How will I handle this?*

It was eight o'clock p.m. as Marc and I sat in silence on one of the two couches in the family room, several feet apart. The mantel clock ticked off the minutes, and the stereo played soft music to keep any conversation we might have from the precious little ears on the floor above us. Twenty minutes passed.

My mind traveled back to my childhood, to the summer between fifth and sixth grade—that oh-so-difficult transitional summer between elementary and middle school. My best friend lived down the street from me. We had shared everything: clothes, secrets, laughter, and tears. We had been friends since kindergarten, and I thought we were inseparable.

One day during that summer as I was riding my bike around the block, I saw her in the street talking with another neighbor friend. I rode closer to hang out with them, and I heard these stinging words from my best friend as she spoke to our neighbor, "Pretend you don't see her, and maybe she won't stop."

Pretend you don't see her, and maybe she won't stop.

I can't remember the bike ride home. I know only that I did not stop, and we never spoke again—never. I had no idea what I might have done to cause my closest friend to hurt me in that way. I started middle school feeling very much alone. Abandoned.

Throughout middle school, I was a nomad, moving from one group to another. First, I spent my time with other athletes. Then, I moved on to the friendly classmates with girl-next-door reputations. They were genuine and fun. I adored them. However, I didn't feel like I fit in anywhere. Everyone else seemed so authentic while I was afraid to be myself. I no longer shared my secrets, dreams, or feelings with anyone. *What if they get to know me and don't like me?* Fear dictated my life.

Finally, I joined the eccentric crowd. There were the kids who kept pet lizards and wrote cryptic poetry. I was already feeling odd; befriending them didn't seem to be such a far stretch. They embraced the peculiar. I loved them for that because that's how I felt. Essentially, I wanted to find friends who would like me forever, ones who would not give up on me or replace me with someone better.

I had turned into a suspicious, worried and very lost teenager on the inside and a tough girl on the outside—tough, but very much alone. Competitive. Determined. Insensitive. I learned how to act as if things didn't bother me. I never cried in the presence of others. I focused on academic and athletic goals rather than relationships. I began to leave a trail of terminated friendships in my path.

That tough facade followed me into high school and college. I wish I had run to God at that point, but I didn't. I ran to boys.

I thought there would be less drama and less competition with male friends, so I ditched the girlfriends and started dating. I continued to live in fear. I ended up hurting others or pushing them away, and for that I feel regret.

So, in my junior year of college, when this unassuming and sincere guy showed some interest in getting to know me better, I was thrilled. We had met two years earlier while trash talking over a basketball game in a mutual friend's dorm room. Then in that third year of school, when another guy across the hall started giving me too much unwanted attention, I asked Marc if he would pretend to be my boyfriend so that this guy would leave me alone. Within a few weeks, we were sitting at the campus pond during the late hours of the night, talking about God. He shared his Christian faith with me and explained what a relationship with Jesus could mean for my life. Our fictitious relationship turned into a real courtship.

We enjoyed each other's company and both seemed to thrive on adventure and active schedules. Marc seemed so confident in his faith and so sure of right versus wrong. He openly cared about people. I watched him put others first. He had masqueraded as my boyfriend to help deter a stalker, and he barely knew me. I felt important. I thought: *I have found him—a safe person, someone who won't abandon me.* We became inseparable. Marc took me to church. He taught me how to read the Bible. I asked tough questions. He was so sure of his answers.

Then one morning, as I sat in my dorm room reading the Bible on my own, it was as if a sledgehammer of understanding hit my soul. I prayed. I cried. In a moment of peace, joy, and excitement, I asked Jesus into my life. I was ready to start over. I was tired of the fear. Becoming a believer allowed me to hand over some of the mess I felt in my life at the time. Messy friendships. Unhealthy dating relationships. Poor decisions. Loneliness. I couldn't wait to share with Marc the decision I had made.

I wish I had known at the time that faith would not seal up all the pain in my life. However, my worries seemed to wash away for a time. I believed Marc, a strong Christian believer, would never hurt me. He was too good. He had introduced me to my Savior! Marc was fun yet sensitive, adventurous yet profound. And now I had God, the Maker of everything on my side, too. I felt unstoppable.

Three years later, we moved to North Carolina and married when we were twenty-three. I felt safe and secure. My fear of abandonment had disappeared. I had no anxiety about being replaced by anyone who might be better. That first year after the wedding, I would have described our marriage as wonderful.

A few more years passed. Little by little, thoughts of nurseries and diapers started to creep into our minds. At one point, I thought I might be pregnant. I wasn't. When that turned out to be more of a disappointment than a relief, we decided we were, in fact, ready to start a family.

A year went by without a positive pregnancy test. My doctor found nothing out of the ordinary with me, so my husband's health was assessed. There were still no red flags—no answers. Two years later, experts in the field of reproduction diagnosed us with "unexplained infertility."

At first, I thought God had abandoned me just like my childhood friends. I thought He had made a mistake and that perhaps He didn't love me as much as I thought He did. I soon realized it was just the opposite. After much prayer, His plan was exposed. It was far better than ours. Marc and I became parents through the miracle of adoption. God is so good.

From Russia with Love
August 29, 2012
Jan 8, 2013 (Revised)
"Yet what we suffer now is nothing compared to the glory He will reveal to us later."
Romans 8:18

Gut-wrenching pain—I know it well. If you or anyone you know has ever suffered through infertility, then you know the heartbreak that couples who are struggling with this issue experience.

My husband and I continued to try to have a baby for almost four years. There were scheduled "date nights" when neither one of us was really in the mood, countless injections of hormones, hot flashes, ultrasounds, pregnancy tests, ovulation kits, test tubes, medical procedures, books, new diets, tears, and yes … many prayers. Our friends didn't know what to say to us. Our family had no idea how to help us. It was really tough. We watched in bittersweet agony as several family members and friends became pregnant and started their own families.

I vividly recall one afternoon when I walked in the house through the garage door to find my husband in emotional shambles.

His tear-streaked face and quaking body startled me, and my mind raced to figure out who must have just died. The good news was that no one had passed away. My husband was brought to his knees by the news that his sister and her husband were expecting their first child. Of course, a part of him was ecstatic for them ... but, a bigger part of him was lost in the unanswered question of "why not us?"

Every morning at five o'clock a.m., I would wake up to sit and pray in the empty room that we had designated for our nursery, just pleading with God. Sometimes I even yelled too. I prayed continuously to get pregnant. I could not understand any of it. Why was God saying "no"?

Finally, after four long years, I relented and changed the content of my prayers. My pleas to get pregnant became prayers of "Your will be done," and "God help me accept whatever you have planned for us." God, ease my grief! Help me live again! That is precisely when I was hit "by the 2x4." On a ten-second walk into a restaurant, God quietly whispered in my ear, "Adopt." It was just one word. A word that had previously been so painful that I refused to hear or say it out loud had become God's answer. It was then that I released my desires and grasped onto God's will.

Seven short months later, my husband and I traveled to Rostov, Russia to bring home our little baby boy. It was our agency's fastest adoption process in history. As our case worker explained that no couple had ever received a referral in just two days, I heard God laughing. God had to hit me with that 2x4 in His perfect timing, and I had to be obedient right there in that restaurant parking lot ... or we would have missed the greatest thing in our lives. We had to trust His will rather than our own as the best course for our lives. Just writing this brings me to tears. Had I not suffered as much as I did for those four years, I never would have relinquished my plan for His plan. I never would have met the little baby waiting for me on the other side of the world … the one who has changed my world forever! God knew this as He was catching every one of my tears during that time of agony.

During the four years we struggled with starting a family, Marc and I shared a pain that brought us even closer, a pain no one else could fully understand. We grew together as we lived through the infertility battle and continued to team up to face each new challenge in our marriage. Throughout each adoption decision and process, I grew closer to God too.

Sitting on that leather couch that night, next to the man who knew me best, who had led me to Christ back in college and jump-started my faith journey, and who had gone through the pain of infertility with me, I felt stunned. The one whom I had trusted with everything had just hurt me more than anyone ever had. He did not seem to be my partner, anymore. He wasn't going to spur on the next fun activity or help me through this challenge. He seemed like my number one enemy.

"I don't know what to say." These were the only words I could speak.

I tried to reconcile the man I thought I had married with the one sitting next to me. I couldn't. I sat there confused as time continued to pass. I was almost certain there was no other pain worse than what I felt at that moment. Several times, I opened my mouth to say something yet nothing came out. Marc was silent.

As Christians, we carry around disappointments, sin, death, and darkness as this world brings us difficult experiences. The significance of Jesus' death on the cross courses through our hearts and souls. He died in our place and for our sins. I thought briefly, *He died for this too.*

I knew this truth that first day after Marc revealed his betrayal. I knew Jesus' victory over death would mean victory over all my heartache and pain. I believed in Jesus' restorative power. I knew intellectually that darkness never wins. However my heart, that night and in the following months, was not on board. A piece of me had died. *How was I ever going to get through this?*

Around eleven p.m., Marc went upstairs to get ready for bed. I followed some distance behind. He brushed his teeth while I sat on the bed. Then, he grabbed a pillow and blanket and went back downstairs to put them on the couch we had just left. I was thankful for this small gesture of discretion. No longer wanting to undress in the same room with him, I certainly did not want to share our bed with him. He had seen me naked thousands of times, but I no longer felt safe and secure. I could not imagine wanting him to look at me *that way* again.

The pain of long-ago abandonment that I had believed to be healed was renewed and amplified with Marc's admission. All I could think about was how he had replaced me—just like my childhood friend had done so many years before. Except this time, the relationship that had been violated is—by God's design—the most intimate one on earth. My good, safe husband had done what I never believed he was capable of doing.

We spoke no more that night. I shut the door to our bedroom to be alone. Before climbing into bed, I searched for my wedding rings. I did not want to put them back on—only to put them away. I did not find them on the floor or in the sofa. Marc had already placed them in my jewelry box at some point that evening. The wedding photo I had torn down was resting against the wall in our closet.

I lay in bed and the first of many waves of tears streamed down my face.

Chapter 3
NINE DAYS

I slept hard that first night and woke up to my two-year-old daughter's stare. She had been an early riser since the day we brought her home from China and called her our own. She was now standing beside my bed, only the top of her head and eyes visible. It was five thirty a.m. on Friday. *TGIF.* Sarcasm slid its way through my mind and into my mood.

I pulled her into the bed. Then, as I did every morning, I turned on the television with the remote I kept bedside and rolled over for another thirty minutes of rest.

At six o'clock a.m., I looked up, prayed for strength, and stood. I helped my little girl get dressed in her own room and then roused my first-grader at seven o'clock. He required extra encouragement to get out of bed and ready for the ride to school. It seemed nothing was going to be easy.

When I came downstairs, I noticed the evidence of Marc's night in the family room was gone. He had already showered, and as I made breakfast I heard him calling in sick to work. He walked into the kitchen and kissed our kids good morning. I could not look him in the eyes. I felt disgust. It was the start of the Labor Day weekend. We had four days before he was to return to work—return to the place with *the other woman*. My anger flared as I thought of her.

I assumed we would try again to talk after lunch while our son was at school and our daughter napped. I did not look forward to it. I had one thing to say before I left with the children for school. "You need to find a counselor."

The admission that he had cheated had revealed a Marc so unlike the Marc I knew. I just wanted him to get some help. My personal circles have always included mental health professionals. Pointing him toward a counselor made sense to me. So as I drove to and from the school, Marc searched online for a Christian therapist for himself. Typically, I handled the family's medical appointments. On this day, I just didn't care who he found or when he went for the session.

Naptime arrived and Marc returned. We sat at the kitchen counter on the two barstools. I asked about the counseling session. I noticed—angrily, silently—that he had chosen a female therapist. She had listened to the parts of the story he was willing to share on an introductory visit but had said little. I was disappointed. I wanted answers, advice … something!

More information did come. I was soon wishing for it to stop. That afternoon was the beginning of nine horrific days of revelations that would forever change my marriage, my faith, my family, and me. Marc began to share small pieces of a secret second life—one he had hidden since before we married. In fact, no one had known about it. Each day brought more shock, anger, and pain to my weary system. Each day it became clearer: *This is more than an affair. It runs much deeper and darker than that.*

Days One and Two. Each morning, I struggled to sit up in bed. My body was heavy with emotional fatigue, my mind felt frozen in time, and I no longer felt secure in my own home. I kept recalling Marc's living room confession. "We had sex." The flashbacks came without warning. Each brought a fresh wave of hurt. I continued to get through each day, hour by hour.

We established a nighttime routine. Once the kids were in bed, Marc and I met on the family room sofa. I sat a few feet away from him, not wanting to be close. We turned on the stereo for background noise. I asked questions. Marc answered. My flowing anger came through in the tone of my voice. His depression and fear showed up in the spaces of silence between my questions and his answers.

This frustrated me immensely—his hesitation to answer. It made me wonder what he was holding back. I felt I deserved answers without having to wait. *Is he forming answers he thinks I want to hear rather than telling me the truth? Is he afraid to tell me everything?* Hindsight tells me there was probably nothing he could have said to change how I felt. He couldn't erase what he had done, the mistakes he had made.

Day Three. As my family ate lunch, I retreated from the kitchen to the master bathroom upstairs. I walked through the front of the bathroom to the small inner room that held just the toilet, shutting the door behind me—grateful for every door I could close between the kitchen and this tiny space. I craved solitude. I did not turn on the light. I curled up in a fetal position on the floor.

I remember feeling the cold tile against my face. I shut my eyes tightly and began to cry. There was not enough toilet paper to soak up my tears. My throat hurt. My eyes hurt. My heart hurt. In the midst of my sobs and shaking, I had a sudden and strange thought: *God will make this good.*

I sat up. I believed the thought. After a few minutes, I dried my eyes and prayed for more strength. I held tight to the promise God had just provided, and I went back downstairs. I was still hiding my pain from our kids.

That evening, I left Marc on the couch in the middle of another long and painful discussion, escaping this time to our bedroom. I grabbed my Bible and sat on the bed. Marc's revelations were mounting, and I was on the brink of kicking him out of the house.

Sex with his co-worker wasn't a one-time thing.

Their relationship had gone on for months.

This was not his first affair.

Two years into our marriage, he had been with a stranger from an online chat room.

That night, as the tears fell onto the pages of the Book of Psalms, I asked God out loud, "What do I do with this?"

My flesh cried out, *Run! Throw him out, collect your precious kids into your arms, and move on.* That is, after all, how I had always believed other women should respond in these types of situations. The vows of marriage promise, " …until death do us part," but I believe the Bible also justifies divorce in cases of infidelity. In the past, I had inwardly applauded wives such as Elin Nordegren when she hammered Tiger Woods' car with a golf club and served him divorce papers. I shook my head in critical judgment at other celebrities' and politicians' wives, such as Hillary Clinton, who chose to stay with unfaithful husbands. I had grown up learning to stand up for and respect myself. Society had taught me over the years: *You deserve more. You can do better.*

Memories of the good parts of our marriage and the confusion that this story was now mine stopped me from changing the locks or driving away with my children. Twice I had gone so far as to write the note: *Here are the keys to my parents' place at the lake. Here is a packed bag. Don't come back into this house.* Twice, I had taped the note to the outside of the garage door while Marc attended counseling sessions. Twice, I had taken it down before he got home. I felt I needed more time, more information, and more direction. I was waiting on God. That night, sitting in bed, asking desperate questions, I felt Him answer. *Don't leave yet.*

Calm and matter-of-fact, the voice that spoke to my heart was not of myself. It was not frantic, as I felt. It was calm. Powerful. Wise. E. Stanley Jones in "A Song of Ascents," writes "We also sense inwardly the immediate *power* of God's voice … The voice of the subconscious argues with you, tries to convince you; but the inner voice of God does not argue, does not try to convince you. It just speaks, and it is self-authenticating." As soon as I recognized the voice of the Lord, I made a decision.

It is difficult to describe the change that occurred in my heart at that moment. I recalled my thought on the bathroom floor earlier that day. *God will make this good.* And as with the flip of a switch, I chose to trust God with every ounce of strength I had left. It was like receiving a life preserver at the instant your nose is about to dip below the waves. I chose to rely on the integrity of God with a confidence I had never known.

I closed my Bible, took a deep breath, slipped off my bed, and walked back downstairs. The words I spoke to the broken man on my couch—the one I had vowed to love through sickness and health—were a surprise even to me.

"You better be a sex addict. It's the only reason I will stay," I said. Then, we sat there in silence for what seemed an eternity.

I had never personally known someone with an admitted sex addiction. I had only heard about it in the context of celebrities and politicians. I did not even know if I believed it existed. To be honest, I knew very little about any kind of addiction. My life had been a sheltered one to this point. I knew from my medical education that addictions changed the brain. I knew they altered the body. I had heard they wrecked lives, too. I was about to learn so much more. Rapid-fire thoughts flooded my mind.

Is he an addict?

Is an addiction an illness?

I promised to stand by him through sickness, not just health.

What am I doing?

I suggested to Marc that he find a new Christian therapist who specialized in sex addiction. His initial choice had been a family therapist. Intuitively, I believed he—we—would need expert help if there was to be any hope of our marriage surviving this darkness. Finding the right counselor became priority number one.

Day Four. I woke up early—before anyone else—and packed a bag. In it were my running shoes, a hat, my Bible, a water bottle, and some snacks. I left a note. *Going to the lake. Don't call.*

My parents, who live several states away, own a second place. It's a condo on a lake near Marc's and my home. I could be alone there. I set out to find some rest. I needed to get away and be with God. I needed to run.

When I arrived, I immediately changed into my running shoes. As I jogged, I cried behind my sunglasses. The people in the cars that passed me in this small college town were heading to church or brunch. They had no idea they were driving past a jogger who wept harder than she ran.

After several miles, I felt exhausted, beat down. I had an overpowering feeling that more bad news was coming. I returned to the condo, picked up my water bottle, and went to the dock. I sat looking out at the water. *God, give me a sign. I don't know what to do. I don't know how much more I can take.* Nothing happened. There was just silence.

Back in the condo, my phone rang. *I told him not to call!* When I looked at the caller ID, I debated whether to answer. It was one of my parents calling. I had not shared what I was experiencing with them. I wasn't ready to share much with anyone. I answered with my best attempt at normal.

"Hey, Cort. I have some bad news." It was my dad. There had been a death in my younger brother's family.

My husband might be a sex addict.

I don't know if my marriage will last.

And my brother's wife had just lost her mother unexpectedly.

I laid my phone down and face-planted into the couch. It was not unlike the first time I buried my head in seat cushions just a few days ago. I let out an aching cry—one that wrapped around the room. I cried for my sister-in-law. I cried for my brother, my nephew, my marriage, my kids, and myself.

I texted Marc to let him know the news. Then I put down my phone and went into one of the bedrooms in the condo and curled into a ball, my knees tucked underneath my chest. My hands cupped my face on the carpet. A return text came back.

"Are you okay?"

"Yes"

For five hours, I stayed on that carpet. I prayed. I pored over the Bible. I sobbed. Finally, I began to miss my children, so I packed up and drove home. I had skipped church. They would be wondering where I was.

Days Five and Six. As Marc searched for a new counselor, he continued to disclose pieces of his secret second life.

There was a third affair.

He can't stop looking at pornography.

This all started before we met.

With every sickening admission, my world narrowed. Little else mattered. My work deadlines went unmet. My social life was put on hold. Life slowed to an aching pace.

Marc returned to work after the holiday weekend. Fear gripped me. I tried not to think about him and his co-worker together in the same office space. Throughout those two days, I experienced a lot of nausea and headaches. In the evenings, I wanted details of every word, look, and encounter between them. There was no trust left. When Marc was home, I required him to leave his cell phone on the kitchen counter. I had collected all of the passwords, and I routinely checked it for any contact with this woman—or any other. Marc knew I was checking in on him. He did not know how frequently, and this caused me to wrestle with some shame of my own. Still, I continued.

I retreated deeper into the only place I found comfort … in God's trustworthy arms.

God's Character: A List that Holds Power (Part II)
November 26, 2013

"For if you remain silent at this time, relief and deliverance for the Jews will arise from another place, but you and your father's family will perish. And who knows but that you have come to your royal position for such a time as this?"
Esther 4:14

I have never done this. I am writing a devotional story before it happens. Not only that, but I want to ask you—the readers—for something. This week, I will be a bit selfish if you will allow it. I am not writing for you but rather asking something of you … prayer. For the next couple weeks, I need heavy, constant, cavernous, and Spirit-filled prayer.

As we look to the Lord as leader of our lives, there will come times when our humanity seems to overpower our hearts. God will ask us to do something that we believe is just too difficult. A battle between flesh and spirit will ensue. When this happens, many of us will have a similar response: Anything but that. We will barter and negotiate. We might even ignore His request altogether.

Those times when we utter the "anything but that" plea expose our faith gaps:

I will do anything but risk my marriage.

I will do anything but lose my dreams.

I will do anything but leave my job.

I will do anything but end this relationship.

I will do anything but give away my money.

I will do anything but give up my health.

I will do anything but release my children to You.

I will do anything but travel there.

I will do anything but … that.

It is so simple to convince ourselves that we are all-in with our faith and lives as His servants until He presents us with that thing. It is easy to speak our willingness to lose everything … until everything must be lost in order to experience the ultimate gain. Will we actually sacrifice for the very One who sacrificed everything for us?

These past two years, I have wrestled with God many times. On each occasion, I have chosen God and died to myself. With each instance, a tremendous amount of joy and more responsibility *have followed. Luke 12:48 in the NIV says, " …From everyone who has been given much, much will be demanded; and from the one who has been entrusted with much, much more will be asked."* I cannot explain the Lord's reasons, but He has entrusted me with much these last two years. I have done my best to obey and follow Him, focusing my eyes on Jesus and basing my decisions on the truths in His Word. In return, more has been asked of me.

With each act of obedience, with each daily death, I am losing this life—the one that is filled with chaos, pain, and fear—and finding life in Him. It is a life filled with abundant joy, peace, and hope. Each flesh death has been worth it; God has made so much good of so much ugly in my life.

So why am I terrified of what He has asked of me next?

It's that thing. It's the pinnacle of all my things. After months of wrestling with God over life-size things and prevailing in that God has fulfilled every one of His promises, God has now offered me the opportunity to surrender the ultimate thing and pick up my heaviest cross. It is the one thing I turn back to gaze on longingly even as I desire to drop everything and follow Christ.

God's character matters to me more today than yesterday. It must. Clinging to His character, I can walk into what I am about to face without fear or anxiety … but will I? So I begin the God-wrestle again, knowing full well that obedience will be worth it. Yet fear still threatens to take hold and attempt to convince me otherwise. Do I trust God with this too? After all I have sacrificed, will He make this good as well? I know the answer in my head. It has been proven in all my past experiences, but my knowledge and discernment have not convinced my heart quite yet.

God has proven His trustworthiness. When the time comes, I need to cling to the whole of His character—that character list. God is forgiving. God is just. God is good. God is steadfast. God is creative. God has integrity.

I don't know how the pieces will fall into place in the next couple of weeks, but I do know God. This is my Esther moment. **"And who knows but that you have come to your royal position for such a time as this?" (Esther 4:14)** *Esther's God-ordained purpose was made evident during a faith gap decision that pitted her very life against the lives of her own people. When she wrestled with God and chose obedience, God saved them all. He was just, good, steadfast, creative, and full of integrity for Esther. He has been for me too.*

My thing *involves life and death on many levels. My thing involves sacred relationships, trust, and forgiveness. It involves swelling emotions, authenticity, truth, grief, and loss. Eternity hangs in the balance. God is near, waiting in expectation. What will I choose?*

What would you choose?

Day Seven. Marc met with a specialist in sexual addiction in our area. I anxiously waited to hear about the session. That evening, after the kids were asleep, Marc shared the details of his appointment, as well as more revelations.

There were poignant stories and secrets from his childhood
He once had a lunch date in our home.
He has been lying uncontrollably throughout our marriage.

The counselor encouraged Marc to join a weekly support group that included education and encouragement for those struggling with sexual addiction. He had also referred me, through Marc, to a spouse's group that met every Wednesday night for ten weeks.

When I heard that, I crumbled onto the floor in a heap of raw emotion. His problem had just become my problem. *How did I get here?* My anger stirred, and I looked from my empty ring finger to the wedding band on his finger. In a fit of rage, I yelled, "I don't even know why you're wearing your wedding ring! You never kept your vows. It disgusts me to look at it on your finger." I stormed up to bed.

Day Eight. It was Friday again. One of the perks of Marc's job was having every other Friday off. While my son was at school and my daughter slept, I found myself sitting on the floor of the family room while Marc shared yet another piece of his double life. The cycle of pain seemed never-ending. As he sat on the couch, I looked up and noticed his empty ring finger.

"Where is your ring?"

"I took it off because you said to. I am just trying to make you happy!"

I almost gave up right then and there. I felt like I was married to a child, one who couldn't understand right from wrong. Marc retreated to our son's bedroom to escape my angry words. As he ran up the steps, an eye-opening glimmer of understanding washed over me. God had just provided me with some insight. I ran after Marc. He was in our son's room making the bed, finding something to do rather than facing me. I stopped in the doorway. My heart raced. My anger turned to deep sadness. Tears welled up. Something now made sense to me. In all the emotional chaos, despite feeling lost and confused, something finally clicked.

In a pleading voice, I spoke wisdom I never realized I knew. "I don't want you to do what will make me happy. I want you to do what is right!" Marc stared at me. It seemed he did not understand what I meant. He did not comprehend that the two are not the same. I left the room to give him time to think about it. I also wanted some time to think.

Day Nine. It was around ten o'clock at night. I was lying on the floor in my master bedroom closet. It seemed when I felt I couldn't handle the stress of all of this hurt, I retreated to the floor. The bathroom floor. The bedroom floor. Now, the closet floor.

I was beginning to question my decision to follow God and see this thing through. Marc was at a support group meeting, and I was scheduled to start mine soon. As I lay there staring at dirty laundry, as if to answer my question, God revealed a Scripture to me that I had struggled with for many years. I suddenly remembered a passage about jars of clay. I ran to my nightstand and grabbed my Bible.

2 Corinthians 4—Present Weakness and Resurrection Life
Therefore, since through God's mercy we have this ministry, we do not lose heart. Rather, we have renounced secret and shameful ways; we do not use deception, nor do we distort the word of God. On the contrary, by setting

forth the truth plainly we commend ourselves to everyone's conscience in the sight of God. And even if our gospel is veiled, it is veiled to those who are perishing. The god of this age has blinded the minds of unbelievers, so that they cannot see the light of the gospel that displays the glory of Christ, who is the image of God. For what we preach is not ourselves, but Jesus Christ as Lord, and ourselves as your servants for Jesus' sake. For God, who said, "Let light shine out of darkness," made his light shine in our hearts to give us the light of the knowledge of God's glory displayed in the face of Christ.

But we have this treasure in jars of clay to show that this all-surpassing power is from God and not from us. We are hard pressed on every side, but not crushed; perplexed, but not in despair; persecuted, but not abandoned; struck down, but not destroyed. We always carry around in our body the death of Jesus, so that the life of Jesus may also be revealed in our body. For we who are alive are always being given over to death for Jesus' sake, so that his life may also be revealed in our mortal body. So then, death is at work in us, but life is at work in you.

It is written: "I believed; therefore I have spoken." Since we have that same spirit of faith, we also believe and therefore speak, because we know that the one who raised the Lord Jesus from the dead will also raise us with Jesus and present us with you to himself. All this is for your benefit, so that the grace that is reaching more and more people may cause thanksgiving to overflow to the glory of God.

Therefore we do not lose heart. Though outwardly we are wasting away, yet inwardly we are being renewed day by day. For our light and momentary troubles are achieving for us an eternal glory that far outweighs them all. So we fix our eyes not on what is seen, but on what is unseen, since what is seen is temporary, but what is unseen is eternal.

Jars of clay.

It was a chapter that I had never fully comprehended but that had intrigued me from the first time I had read it many years ago. I pored over it again there in the closet. As I did, an amazing thing happened: I finally understood it. No—I didn't just understand it; I felt like the words were written just for me. Recalling the experience reminds me of Hebrews 4:12, which says:

"For the word of God is alive and active. Sharper than any double-edged sword, it penetrates even to dividing soul and spirit, joints and marrow; it judges the thoughts and attitudes of the heart."

I felt my soul and spirit divide in that closet. I was fiercely moved. I held the Bible tightly against my chest. *This is my life verse. There is purpose here.* I stood up from the closet with a renewed sense of strength. God's Word had just restored some of my depleted energy. I still felt drained, but I now had a glimpse of how God might make this mess of a marriage into something good.

"Therefore we do not lose heart. Though outwardly we are wasting away, yet inwardly we are being renewed day by day. For our light and momentary troubles are achieving for us an eternal glory that far outweighs them all."

Hope was born in my closet that night. Yes, I was a fragile clay jar with a crack that was threatening to shatter my soul. However, God was here. He was holding me together with super-glue strength. I promised myself to fix my eyes on Jesus and not on my current circumstances. This pain was merciless … and temporary. I wouldn't lose heart. God was doing something here.

It seemed I had turned a corner. Earlier that day, with his last reveal, Marc promised that he had finally told me everything he could remember. I believed him. I believed him only because he qualified it with "that I can remember." It was not an absolute statement. It was his truth, as he knew it. I finally knew what I was dealing with in this marriage of ours.

Chapter 4
MY HIDING CAVE

"David left Gath and escaped to the cave of Adullam..."
—1 Samuel 22:1

Following those nine dark days, it seemed everything started to happen at once. It was up and down for several weeks. I would feel unexpectedly strengthened and hopeful for a time, and then just as quickly, be brought to tears once again. I began to realize that healing—in whatever form God intended—was going to be a long process. Marc's initial admission and the reveal process had taken its toll on me.

The pain was physical. I had lost my appetite and dropped a few pounds. Severe headaches emerged every afternoon. Aches and pains I had never before experienced ruled my waking hours. Instead of playing with my daughter on the floor, I would lie next to her while she fiddled with her toys. My shoulders. My neck. My heart. They all hurt.

The pain was spiritual. Satan taunted me daily. During the first nine days, I had struggled exclusively with anger and shock. Now, the demon of self-doubt crept in.

This is your fault.

If you had shown more interest in sex, he wouldn't have gone elsewhere.

How could you not see the clues?

Your husband doesn't find you attractive.

The other women were better.

The lies came fast and furious. I looked in the mirror and analyzed my body. There was no flattery involved. I unfairly critiqued every part of myself. Suddenly, my athletic build seemed too "boyish." I began to long for curves in places I had never wanted them before. I even thought about cutting my hair. I wondered, *Am I attractive to anyone?*

Ephesians 6:12 states, "For our struggle is not against flesh and blood, but against the rulers, against the authorities, against the powers of this dark world and against the spiritual forces of evil in the heavenly realms." During this time, this Scripture took on a whole new level of meaning in my life. I was struggling daily.

The Holy Spirit within me would not allow me to believe the lies for long. Louder and more powerful was the voice of truth.

This is not your fault.

God loves you.

You are beautiful.

God has this.

Trust Him.

This will not define you—or your marriage—when God is finished here.

Within a week, the self-doubt slowly disappeared. I was reminded that I was made in God's image—wonderfully made. No person or circumstance can take that from me.

One night, I experienced an intense dream that left me shaken. In my dream, I was lying in bed in the dark, and Marc was in our master bathroom a few feet away. The bathroom light was on. Next to the bed, I felt a dark and evil presence lingering. I knew in my heart that a demon was standing there—next to the bed. The sensation was so intense. In my dream, I wanted to be able to put shape to the demon so I sat up and quickly threw my sheets and blankets over the presence—to give it a form I could see. It worked. Sure enough, my sheets landed on a vile shape that exuded anger. Fear set in, and I scrambled off the bed, struggling to get to the light of the bathroom and out of the darkness of the bedroom. Crawling quickly, I had just about reached the doorway when the demon grabbed my leg and started to pull me back into the darkness. I clawed my way toward the light, trying to scream. No sound came out.

Then I woke up. A cold sweat soaked my clothes and sheets. I lay in my bed, heart pounding, body paralyzed by my dream. I tried to pray. At first, my lips wouldn't move, but I sensed I had to say the words out loud. *If I can just say "Jesus," it will flee.* I had to speak that name and not just think it, yet it was so difficult to open my mouth. It felt as if someone had injected Novocain into my lips. Fear struggled for the win. It didn't: "Jesus."

The fear vanished. The air in my bedroom became lighter. I knew evil had left. I believe my obedience to God's request to fight for my marriage threatened Satan's plans. I had made a choice to follow God into His light and try to make this marriage work despite the odds against it. Perhaps, the devil wasn't happy.

The pain was emotional. Worse than the physical pain was the onslaught of mental images. My mind's eye was inundated with scenes of Marc with other women. I didn't even know what some of them looked like—it didn't matter. I would be drying my hair in front of my mirror, and suddenly imagine him with his co-worker. I would be driving down the road and recall in vivid detail my guttural scream on Day One. When that particular image flooded my head, my body reacted physically as well. My heart rate would spike and nausea would overtake me. These flashbacks, as a counselor would later call them, occurred several times a day, rendering me useless during the episodes. My planning skills suffered. I could not think ahead. My mind seemed to slow down. I would hear the voices of my children or co-workers when they spoke to me, but I could not process the meaning of their words. My memory experienced lapses that were not characteristic of my usually type-A, well-organized personality.

One early evening during that second week after the initial disclosure, I went for a walk in our neighborhood. During the entire three-mile loop I talked to God. The prayers were pleas for God to take away the images. *God, I cannot keep reliving these moments. Please, Lord, take them away. I need a break.* God answered my prayers. For twenty-four hours, the flashbacks and images ceased. My brain rested and my hope grew.

> "So we fix our eyes not on what is seen, but on what is unseen, since what is seen is temporary, but what is unseen is eternal." (2 Corinthians 4:18, in the NIV)

The following day, an image reappeared, and I immediately asked God to fill my head with something good. I prayed the words in Philippians 4:8, and Satan fled, taking the horrible image with him. The passage became a daily prayer, and the images' frequency lessened to monthly taunts rather than the daily deluge I had been experiencing.

> "Finally, brothers and sisters, whatever is true, whatever is noble, whatever is right, whatever is pure, whatever is lovely, whatever is admirable — if anything is excellent or praiseworthy — think about such things." (Philippians 4:8, in the NIV)

Then came an elevated distrust of all men. If *my* husband could do something like this, then every husband must be doing it. Irrational fears and assumptions reigned. One day as I drove through my neighborhood, I saw a young couple out running together on the sidewalk. Remembering my routine runs with Marc before children entered our lives, I immediately assumed this husband was hiding something. *They look so happy; it can't be real.* I had become jaded and paranoid.

A few weeks after Marc's initial disclosure, I made an appointment with my gynecologist to be tested for sexually transmitted diseases. When I called my doctor's office, I could barely talk—a sob of humiliation and dread sat deep in my throat. My regular doctor was on vacation, so I was asked to choose another. "I want a female doctor, please." My face was hot with shame. Tears spilled as I hung up the phone. *I shouldn't have to do this.*

On the day of my appointment, I asked Marc to meet me there so he could watch our daughter in the waiting room while I went back to see the doctor. The drive to the medical complex took my daughter and me on an interstate. A few miles from our exit, the semi truck in front of us blew a tire.

The world became a slow motion film. The ripped tire rose into the air, and I swerved onto the rumble strip to avoid a windshield-to-tire collision. When I swerved, my car's left tires came off the road, and I felt us riding on only two rolling spheres of rubber. My heart leapt into my throat. I blinked and prayed. My daughter, sleeping in the backseat, was blessedly oblivious. The truck's tire hit the left side of my front bumper, and we proceeded to drop back down onto four wheels and run over the truck's lost piece of tire. The semi kept trucking along, and I followed it until my exit. I drove … and I waited. I was sure I would hear the thumping sound indicating a flat tire. As I waited, I thanked God for His protection.

A few minutes later, my mind returned to where I was headed. The shock and numbness regarding my current home situation sank back in, and when I arrived at the parking garage of the medical complex, the drive there had vanished from my mind. I had completely forgotten about our harrowing escape and about any damage to my car that may have occurred. Emotional pain can do that—make everything else in your life dim in comparison.

The next morning as I walked into the garage to take my son to school, I recalled the eighteen-wheeler's blown tire—only because I found a broken headlight and moderate damage to the front of the car. My outer life kept rambling on, even as my inward thoughts and emotions remained in turmoil. I was sure I was losing my mind. I needed a hiding place—a place I could go and remember that God would not let this destroy me.

My absolute favorite person in the Bible—aside from Jesus, of course—is David. For me, David epitomizes the weak but faithful follower who trusts God in a way that elevates him to a mighty warrior. However, David later falls to an envious adversary, forcing him to hide for his life. From caves, he cries out to God. God redeems him and brings him out from the darkness of the caves to re-establish him as one of the most remembered kings of His people. But the story doesn't end there. David was human. He falls again—this time to temptation. God forgives David and re-elevates him to a sacred position in eternity. *Wow!*

In those caves where David hid from his enemy, King Saul, he wrote some of the most powerful, spirit-filled, and memorized psalms in the Bible, including Psalm 57:1 (NIV).

"Have mercy on me, my God, have mercy on me, for in you I take refuge. I will take refuge in the shadow of your wings until the disaster has passed."

Just like David of so long ago, I had found a hiding place. That last night of the nine-day reveal process, as I clutched the Bible and sat on my closet floor, I realized this space would be my cave—the place where I would hide and take refuge to be with God.

Over the next few months, I spent countless hours in there—day and night. I sat and kneeled among the shoes and dirty laundry. Sometimes, I would drop to my knees, put my head on the ground, turn, and stare into the white paint of the baseboards. As I stared, I pictured myself being enveloped by massive feathered wings, large enough to cover my entire body. I pictured God making His wings a cave within my cave, a place for me to hide and weep. Outside, I felt lost, helpless, and full of despair. Under His wings, I felt safe, hopeful, and strengthened.

"When my glory passes by, I will put you in a crevice in the cliff and cover you with my hand until I have passed by." (Exodus 33:22, in the NIV)

That is how I felt in that hiding closet, under God's caring wings. I believed God was protecting me, shielding me with His glorious hand as He worked to make this mess good. In that cave, I learned to trust Him like never before. I rested there, knowing in my heart that He was covering me while

He was passing by, on His way to redeeming my marriage … and my life.

> "He will cover you with his feather, and under his wings you can hide. His truth will be your shield and protection." (Psalms 91: 4, in the NCV)

As my drama unfolded, there were times when I sensed God working overtime to ensure things would turn out good. I began to focus on His eternal plans and promises, and continued to lean on 2 Corinthians 4 as my guide.

> "But we have this treasure in jars of clay to show that this all-surpassing power is from God and not from us. We are hard pressed on every side, but not crushed; perplexed, but not in despair; persecuted, but not abandoned; struck down, but not destroyed. We always carry around in our body the death of Jesus, so that the life of Jesus may also be revealed in our body. For we who are alive are always being given over to death for Jesus' sake, so that his life may also be revealed in our mortal body. So then, death is at work in us, but life is at work in you."

This world will always have a life and death balance system. Brian McLaren wrote in "The Secret Message of Jesus," "What if our only hope lies in this impossible paradox, the only way the kingdom of God can be strong in a truly liberating way is through a scandalous, noncoercive kind of weakness; the only way it can be powerful is through astonishing vulnerability; the only way it can live is by dying." I held onto that message: Death for life's sake.

In my cave, I began to understand that the support group Marc's counselor had recommended was necessary for my healing. I also began to realize the need for me to reach out to a few friends for encouragement, wisdom, and discernment. God impressed upon my heart that this was not something I could handle alone. I would need women of faith to walk alongside me on this tough road, pointing up when it seemed all I could do was fall down.

Chapter 5
"CO-ADDICT"

am a private person. So when Marc's new counselor initially recommended that I attend a support group for spouses of sex addicts, my insides twisted. *What? Admit I am married to a sex addict? Tell strangers what has happened? Say my marriage is a failure?* It took every ounce of God's strength and grace within me to walk through those doors that first Wednesday night, just two raw weeks after Day One.

I stepped into an old Victorian home that had been renovated and transformed into offices. I struggled with conflicting emotions. Part of me felt hollow, defeated. Another part of me was desperately angry. It was an anger born from fear. My marriage was not what I thought it had been, and I still wasn't sure if it was going to survive.

Somehow I sensed I needed to be there, but I was fighting the reality of it every step of the way. For me, a stride through

43

the doors would mean I had failed. It would signify that I had chosen poorly when it came to my life partner. It would reveal that my world had been turned upside down, and I didn't know how to fix it. My independent and proud nature hated the whole idea of a support group, even a Christian one.

Following the directions of the counselor who greeted me, I sat in a chair in the waiting area, clutching my bag. She left the room. After a few minutes, another woman walked in and sat in the chair opposite me. I half-smiled, half-cringed. It was my way of saying, *Hello … I don't want to be here.* She smiled back without any hesitation. "Hi." It seemed too cheerful for the circumstances. I had expected the other women here to feel more like I did—embarrassed and confused. I remember thinking: *Why is she so composed?*

Another woman entered. I guessed her to be about my age. Our eyes briefly met, and I knew in an instant her anguish was as fresh as mine. The shocked, glazed-over look gave her away. She nodded at me, then sat in a third chair and stared at the floor.

The counselor who was leading the group came back into the lobby and invited us into her office. The full group of women arrived. No one spoke once they had introduced themselves to the counselor. Each seemed to pretend no one else was in the room. I looked around. The lamps gave off a muted yellow light. There was a couch and several arm chairs. The seating had been placed in a circle. I assumed the counselor wanted people to feel comfortable in this space. I didn't.

I sat there in my newly claimed seat. I had strategically chosen the single wing chair off to the side rather than the couch, which I would have had to share with others. I knew by their presence here that these women had experienced one of the worst pains a wife could endure. I was still struggling to understand how I had married someone who would commit adultery, and not just once, but repeatedly. I continued to fantasize that this kind of story was only to be told by others. Denial. I had experienced the pain these women had, but I didn't want to become one of them.

I tried to assess the other women. Seven wounded hearts, apart from me. Several acted anxious. They bounced their legs or wrung their fingers. Others seemed comfortable. The one woman who had nodded to me in the lobby appeared how I felt—withdrawn, broken. A tear slipped down her cheek. I tried to look stoic, unmoved by my circumstances. On the inside, however, I was weeping too. *How am I going to share the most sacred parts of my marriage and my intimate feelings with these women?* Rapid-fire thoughts played over and over in my head.

How did I end up here?
This is not me.
Why are there so many women in this place?
This cannot be my life!

That first long night, the counselor led us in an opening prayer. Then each of us shared an overview of why we were sitting in that room.

Our counselor started us off. She was divorced. Her ex-husband was a sex addict. Her story, while different in the details, was like mine. I could not decide if her background brought me any comfort or not. She would understand me because she had experienced similar pain. However, did it leave her jaded or biased?

The first participant began her story. *She can't be more than twenty-five years old,* I thought. She explained that after eleven months of faithfulness, her husband of six years had returned to adultery. My heart sank with sorrow, quickly followed by fear. *Would I face the same situation a year down this terrible road?*

The painful stories continued. Midway through the evening, the counselor said something that sparked anger in me. "You are all co-addicts."

What?!

"And," she asked the group, "What are you addicted to?"

A woman who had participated in the support group before answered, "Our husbands." She was repeating the ten-week session in an effort to find closure after her separation from her husband.

"Right," came the therapist's confirmation. She explained that co-addiction is a very specific type of co-dependency that refers to the relationship between our addict spouses and us. Co-addicts depend on the needs of, or control of another. They place a lower priority on their own needs and desires, while being excessively concerned with the opinions of their spouses. In fact, she explained that for those of us sitting in her office that night, the decision to let go of our addicted spouses is difficult, if not impossible. She said that we didn't put appropriate expectations in place within our marriages to ensure a healthy balance.

I felt my face flush and my heart rate quicken. I was sure that I carried no responsibility for my husband's reckless choices. Yet the term "co-addict" seemed to indicate that I was just as much at fault as Marc. It also seemed that she was supporting separation from our spouses, and even recommending it to those of us who were still living with ours. It had been difficult just to walk through the door that night. These tragic tales and pointed fingers seemed too much to handle.

You can't label me like that! I was not ready to offer much in the way of personal information to this group of strangers, and now the counselor had just left me with an intense first impression that I could not trust her as an unbiased or wise coach.

I went home furious and convinced I would not return to the next session. I spent the week researching co-addiction, sex addiction, spouses of addicts, and any other phrases that Google and Bing recommended I search. I took every online assessment I could find to see if my computer would spit out the same "diagnosis" that this counselor had rushed to stamp on my file. Some of the self-doubt I had struggled with in the prior week returned. *What could I have done differently?*

I sped-read a few books, as well, skimming the chapters for signs that I might be a co-addict, that somehow I was in just as much need of counseling—and fixing—as my husband. Everything came back "no." The results seemed to indicate I did keep healthy boundaries and I was not living with the purpose of ensuring my husband was happy. I was a truth-teller, not a peacekeeper.

I retreated to my hiding cave to find God. I talked to Him often. *God, this isn't my fault, right?* I vowed to myself that I would not accept this label—the one of co-addict—just because a professional counselor had characterized me as such while I sat in a room I had never anticipated finding myself. I did not have to accept the nametag of "Co-Addict" that almost everyone else in the Victorian House seemed to be content to apply to their shirts the moment they walked in and sat down.

As the week of research and doubt went by, I attended a second gathering of godly women. However, this one was much different than the Christian support group. God was going to use this second group to build me up and open my eyes to His unending love for me as I walked down this painful road, providing me with the spiritual strength and affirmation I would need to move forward.

Prior to Marc's initial admission, I had slipped into a spot on a women's ministry team through God's mighty Providence. Initially, I was invited to participate in a "book club" within a women's small group. However after the book discussion ended, the ladies revealed to me a ministry they had recently started. The ministry's mission was to see women rebuilt, restored and renewed in their faith walks with Christ. They asked me if I wanted to be a part of it; the founder shared her belief that God had placed me there for a specific reason. I had no idea what being a member of a ministry team meant or what exactly God was planning. I did know that these women seemed genuine and within the first few hours, I was able to see how much they loved Jesus. Their lives were focused on knowing God and living life for Him.

During worship at the first meeting before Marc's disclosure, the ladies became lost in the songs they sang. No one seemed to remember there were nine of us in the room. It was all about God. Hands were raised. Knees hit the floor. Tears were shed—

all for Jesus. I witnessed what it meant to put God first. When the music ended, I felt what it was like to be loved by a God who was after *me*. I felt Him calling me back—back to His arms after too much time away, trying to do life on my own. I wanted more of that.

It seemed God knew the gut-punch my life was about to receive. He knew my dependence on Him was not strong enough. I was already in a spiritual crisis and didn't even know it. He knew I would need these women to open my eyes to His love for me. So, as He most likely had hoped, I said yes to the invitation to join the ministry team.

The ministry meetings were scheduled monthly. In between that first gathering where I said yes to joining the team and the second meeting a month later, my marriage fell apart. Marc's admission of his multiple affairs rocked me to my core. Yet, in God's perfect plan, He had just surrounded me with eight new Sisters in Christ who knew what it meant to live for Him and be obedient to His word. I would need every one of them, along with a couple other intimate friends, in order to survive the next six months.

At that second meeting with the ministry team, I sat slumped on the couch. I felt rigid, frozen in pain. I crossed my arms in front of my body as if I was hugging myself. The founder of the ministry, Dawn, stopped the discussion midway through the evening and looked at me. In her direct and confident way, she asked, "What's going on? Let's hear it."

It seemed my attempt to be stoic had worked in the support group, but I couldn't pull it off with this group. I relented and let my guard down. My body started shaking, and I squeezed my hands in agony. Through sobs and tremors, I explained to these women of faith whom I had just met a month before that my husband had betrayed me. I shared everything from the pornography addiction to the affairs. As I choked out my story, one by one, they reached for me. Placing their hands on my knees, shoulders, and head, they comforted me with their touch. No one said much, but I could tell they cared deeply. A few cried alongside me. They prayed for me and consoled me.

Almost immediately, they began affirming my decision to work on restoring my marriage. They told me how brave, strong, and faithful I was to attempt to make it work. It was the polar opposite message I had received at the support group. These precious women—for that is certainly what they were— seemed to answer all my questions and alleviate my fears with biblical messages and wise advice before I even expressed them.

Yes, the work of restoring your marriage is the hard road to choose.

God doesn't send us down the easy paths.

You are beautiful and loved.

God is faithful.

God is bigger than this.

You are not alone.

Me too …

Me too? A few of the ministry team members knew my pain first-hand. They, too, had experienced life with an addict. Divorce. Fear. Betrayal. Abandonment. God had been faithful in each of their lives too.

The women on the ministry team gave me a new name: Meira. It means "One Who Illuminates." They were affirming for me that God's hope, love, and light were visible through me despite the hurt. Joy was coming.

One Who Illuminates
July 11, 2012
"We now have this light shining in our hearts, but we ourselves are like fragile clay jars containing this great treasure. This makes it clear that our great power is from God, not from ourselves."
2 Corinthians 4:7 (NLT)

Some of my closest girlfriends gave me a new name ... a Hebrew name, Meira. It means, "one who illuminates." These wonderful Christian women view me as the "Light" of our group. There are nine of us in this accountability group, and each has her own significant name, apart from her birth name. Some of the names are Ariel or "Lion of God," Rafaela or "Healed by God," Cherut or "Freedom," and Liron or "My Song."

These names are a reflection of how a Holy Creator designed us as uniquely as He did each snowflake that falls from the sky. The names also highlight our God-inspired strengths. They represent the holy piece of God that we carry around on display for others to see.

I love my name. It was given to me during a very dark time in my life. It was a reminder of God's truth and His promises. I may be a fragile jar made of clay where life's trials and struggles can crack my exterior and bring me to my knees. However, the Holy Spirit within me is a light that can shine forth through those cracks, spreading love, hope, and truth.

My cracks won't cause me to crumble. My difficult days won't cause me death. Even more amazing than what the Lord does for my heart is how He can use my imperfections and struggles to minister to others. I can be sitting in my own dark cave, and I can still shine with His Light for those around me. I may be ripping at the seams, yet I can still provide to others that same love, hope, and truth that the Lord provides for me.

That is the glory of it all. God is bigger than any of our cracks. He is bigger and better. His power is infinitely stronger than our flesh and the enemy's tactics combined. As 2 Corinthians 4:7 states, "We now have this light shining in our hearts, but we ourselves are like fragile clay jars containing this great treasure. This makes it clear that our great power is from God, not from ourselves." That great treasure is God himself … How does He shine through you? Is it through worship and praise? Is it through ministering to wounded hearts or breaking down walls? Perhaps it is through speaking like a Holy megaphone, teaching others about His message of salvation. For me, it is shining his Light into darkness, illuminating the path for others who may be in trapped in darkness so that they too can see.

After a week of research and prayer and some much-needed encouragement from the ministry team, I began to feel confident that I could discern from the support group what information related to emotional healing would be useful. I would use it in combination with the strength and spiritual healing provided from the ministry team. All this feedback and counsel, if paired with wisdom from God, might give me some guidance toward ultimate healing.

My prayers fueled most of my confidence. God knew me. He knew my story, my heart, and my thoughts. I felt affirmed through Him. I also wanted to do everything I could to try to save this marriage. Yet, I wanted to move forward cautiously. That qualification in my newly found determination was not only my fear speaking, it was prudence. I knew it would be okay to leave the marriage if I felt it was time. That self-permission bolstered my conviction that I was not a co-addict.

Another reason I decided to return to the support group was because I trusted Marc's addiction counselor enough to return. After each session that Marc attended, he shared many of the exchanges between him and his counselor. It was evident that his therapist was not going to allow Marc to side step past his lies, his responsibility, his pain, or his need to start making better decisions. He routinely called Marc out on his deceptions, stopping him in mid-sentence and asking him to start over. Sex addicts don't just start truth telling once they admit the infidelity. It's a long process to relearn how to make decisions and avoid the lies that were used to simplify situations. While I no longer trusted Marc, I trusted this specialist with my husband's recovery. I trusted his recommendations for my healing too. I returned to the Victorian home the next week.

That second Wednesday night, I was again the first to arrive to the support group. This was purposeful. I quickly sat in the same chair that provided me some space from the others. The session began with prayer and then a call for questions. My heart was pounding. I raised my hand. I explained that I did not agree with the statement that we were all co-addicts.

I laid out my case. My self-esteem does not come from how happy my husband feels. My sense of worth and confidence comes from an internal satisfaction from doing my best and the knowledge that I am loved by God. The main focus of my marriage was not to try to figure out what Marc wanted, and then give it to him. I did not constantly worry about what he was thinking about me. Up until his admission, I had never worried about him abandoning me at all. I did not believe I controlled him or enabled him.

The counselor nodded and smiled. I knew that response. She was appeasing me. It seemed she believed she knew everything about me. I became frustrated. Then, something happened that likely prevented me from walking out the door for good.

"I agree with Cortney."

It was the woman who had seemed as full of disbelief and pain as me, the one with whom I had felt a secret but kindred connection on the first night. The one who's glazed over look spoke volumes about how I felt. "I don't think I have any characteristics of a co-addict either."

I had found an ally. We locked eyes, and I stayed in my chair for the remainder of the evening.

I Don't Believe …
January 22, 2013
"You gave me life and showed me kindness, and in your providence watched over my spirit."
Job 10:12

I don't believe in coincidences.

According to Google, a coincidence is "a remarkable concurrence of events or circumstances without apparent causal connection." *Did you know that the word coincidence is not found anywhere in the Bible? I know. I looked in five different translations. It seems to me God doesn't believe in coincidences either. I can't think of any other reason there's absolutely no mention of it in the Bible—the God-inspired book where Scripture* "is alive and active. Sharper than any double-edged sword, it penetrates even to dividing soul and spirit, joints and marrow; it judges the thoughts and attitudes of the heart." *(Hebrews 4:12)*

Sometimes, I think we exchange miracles for coincidences and miss out on God's amazing grace in our lives. We call answered prayers simply "luck" and dismiss our Creator's loving gifts. Some of us have averted our eyes and missed God's providence, choosing to believe in pure happenstance. In the past, I know I have mistaken His provision for mere fate. When we make these perspective choices, I think we ignore a huge part of the amazing relationship God seeks to have with us.

I would like to share with you two "coincidences" to one very specific prayer …

I heard the taunting. It was that voice in my head—the one that is not very complimentary. It's the voice that tears me down, rekindles my fears, and speaks anything but words of encouragement. Do you hear that voice too? His name is Satan.

I knew it was him the moment it started. I began to feel "not good enough." I started to question why I was writing talks for church ministries and wondering who was I to be posting devotional blogs and writing a book. I started to ask myself questions like, "Why do I believe I am making any difference at all?" Thankfully, I recognized the enemy's voice and started to pray against it.

"God, I know you have a plan for me. I know these feelings of 'not good enough' are just attacks—ones meant to strip me of my confidence. I will not bow down to the lies. But, God, I need some confirmation from You. I need You to show me that I am writing messages that are good enough for Your will to be done. I need to know You are here as I pen out these devotionals and these talks. If You could just show me that I have impacted one person for You—just one—then I will know I am supposed to continue on this path," *I prayed.*

I told my husband about the enemy's taunts and how they were getting worse. I confided in him that I was nervous that one of my upcoming talks wasn't going to be good enough—wasn't going to impact anyone in the way I hoped. I shared with him that I wanted it to be perfect so that God could use me to make a difference. His reply was, "Of course the taunts are worse—you are getting dangerously close to not only living your life completely for God, but helping others do the same." *He was right.*

The next day, I was in the middle of the Esther Bible Study by Beth Moore. I read these words and fell flat on my face and cried:

"Beloved, do we believe that the only way to do something acceptable is to do it perfectly? Sometimes God is more aware than we of just how much He requires of us. He knows how hard it's going to be for us … He's proud of us for fighting overwhelming human emotions to do His will." *Praise You, God! The exact thing I had asked God for as confirmation was just handed to me by Him the very next day!*

But God wasn't finished yet. The second day, several individuals—people whom I was not even aware were reading my blog—thanked me for one of my recent posts. These friends' encouragements were more answered prayer. Not only had God told me that I was good enough and reminded me that I didn't have to be perfect, He gave me the confirmation I needed that others were being touched by my blog. Just as with Job, God was watching over me. "You gave me life and showed me kindness, and in your providence watched over my spirit." *My spirit was being tested, but God showed me He was there and reminded me of His kindness.*

Was it coincidence that "Isaac prayed to the LORD on behalf of his wife, because she was childless. The LORD answered his prayer, and his wife Rebekah became pregnant." *(Genesis 25:21)*

Was it coincidence that "David built an altar to the LORD there and sacrificed burnt offerings and fellowship offerings. Then the LORD answered his prayer in behalf of the land, and the plague on Israel was stopped." *(2 Samuel 24:25)*

Was it also coincidence that I asked God for confirmation, and within forty-eight hours, the Lord answered my prayer—twice over?

I refuse to live in a way that would shun God's grace. I refuse to reject God's little gifts. Some people may call these events "coincidences." I believe those who do are missing out on one of the most beautiful aspects of connecting with a Heavenly Father who loves us beyond imagination.

So, here is my new definition of a coincidence: "A coincidence is a set of events (aka blessings) orchestrated by God for His divine purpose but whose recipient refuses to accept as gifts from God, thereby (sadly) choosing to believe fate, rather than Providence, is a more powerful force in his or her life."

While hiding in my cave and then exiting for short spans of time to lean on my Christian friends, I began to understand better that my marriage—all my life's challenges—had left cracks in me. As a fragile clay jar, God was providing me with every kind of support I needed in order to hold me together. A support group for my emotional health. A ministry team for my spiritual health. Friends for my relational health. I felt that God wanted this marriage to survive, but perhaps more importantly, He wanted me to find His purpose for me. God created me for a reason—a holy reason. He alone had the power to hold me together, and He would ensure His light would shine through, despite the pain I was experiencing.

> "We now have this light shining in our hearts, but we ourselves are like fragile clay jars containing this great treasure. This makes it clear that our great power is from God, not from ourselves." (2 Corinthians 4:7, NLT)

I soon realized that I just had to trust God and let go of my desire to hide in my cave forever. So, I continued to walk through those Victorian House doors every Wednesday evening for the remaining eight weeks.

Chapter 6
THE WORK OF LOVE

As the days turned to weeks, I faithfully attended my Wednesday night support group meetings. At times, it was difficult. Marc would arrive home from work, we would rush to eat together as a family, and then I would run out the door as the dishes were being cleared.

I despised that Marc's choices had forced me to miss so many bedtime routines and good night kisses with my children. I despised driving thirty minutes through rush hour traffic to park at the back of that Victorian home. I despised walking in the door as the sun had already set. The Thanksgiving and Christmas holidays were approaching. I was not feeling very merry. Rather, I was still harboring a lot of hate.

I desperately tried to do everything "by the book." I didn't want anyone to blame me for anything. I feared that if I were not successful on my end of the healing process, my marriage would not last. I did not want to end up staring at divorce papers, becoming just another statistic.

My love for Marc was tested during this time. I questioned the existence of unconditional love, wondering if there was such a thing between two people. Or, perhaps unconditional love was only possible from God. I no longer felt love for Marc during this time. I did not think it had simply vanished. We had been married for so many years and had been through so much together. During the next few months, I forced myself to remember what it felt like to love my husband and act accordingly with the prayers that I would one day find that feeling again.

I contemplated my swirling emotions and was forced to name them with each support group session. I was grieving intensely. Almost as if I was viewing myself from above, I had watched my heart go through the first few steps of the grief process—from the shock, numbness, and denial to the deep anger. On the advice from the support group counselor, I kept a journal, beginning each entry with how I felt in that moment, moving to what those feelings caused me to think, and finally writing down how those thoughts affected my actions.

I feel angry. In my anger, I think I may not be able to forgive Marc. When I think I may not be able to forgive Marc, I become sarcastic in order to hide my fear that our marriage will not survive.

Living out my rage those first months, I had become overly sarcastic. I spewed blame everywhere. The root of sarcasm in the Greek is "sarkasmos" and means, "to tear the flesh." That seemed fitting. I wanted my words to cut and wound Marc.

"Why don't you discuss that with your girlfriend."

"So, is the grass greener?"

"Why not share our inside jokes with her? You gave away everything else."

At one point, I described myself to the support group as a "white hot mess." The other women nodded their understanding. Dallas Willard, in his book *Hearing God*, writes, "Through words, soul impacts soul, sometimes with great spiritual force. As marks or sounds alone, words are nothing. It is their mental side, their spiritual force, that hooks into the hidden levers of mind and reality and gives them their immense power." The words of my husband, the words from the counselor, the words I chose to share with others—they all held power. I wondered what that power would accomplish.

Along with anger came anguish. No wife should experience the feelings of betrayal from the most important person in her life.

I feel violated. When I feel like this, I think this work of restoration is too difficult. I can't try to work on a marriage that has been destroyed in this way—so intimately. When I think the marriage won't last, I find it difficult to look Marc in the eye or be in the same room with him.

I felt dishonored, as if other women had been spying on the most intimate moments in my marriage. Yet, I did not want to just give up. I struggled to balance hatred and love, fury and sorrow, regret and hope. One spouse of a sex addict, who was quoted in the workbook the support group used, said this, "Every time I thought about the possibility of having to end the marriage, something inside of me groaned in anguish." I underlined that statement several times in my book. I related to it. I believed the Holy Spirit was the source of that groaning. As I understand it, marriage is a sacred bond designed by God and not created by man. The thought of divorce made me queasy. Yet the thought of marriage with someone I could not trust and who had tarnished our intimacy was just as nauseating.

I continued to hang onto that last word I heard spoken to my heart as I sat on my bed on Night 3, the "out" that God provided when He said, "Don't leave yet." *Yet* ...

I feel hopeless. When I feel hopeless, I assume Marc is the one not trying hard enough. When I think he is not giving this marriage everything he has, I yell at him and walk out of the room, abandoning him so that he can't abandon me.

Marc remained distant—emotionally and spiritually. He had not voluntarily returned to our bed at night. I had not asked him to either. He was still deeply troubled, processing his past mistakes, and trying to heal. I was still livid. It was becoming clearer with each passing week: This was going to be a long process. I wondered how it would end. Romans 8:28 in the NIV promises, "And we know that in all things God works for the good of those who love him, who have been called according to his purpose." It is one of God's promises I fiercely held in the forefront of my mind as we worked on communicating, processing, and healing. *God is working. It will be good.*

Marc and I continued to meet in the evenings on the family room couch. We discussed some of what we had learned in each of our support groups and in his private counseling sessions. Any transformation he was undergoing seemed slow. It created added tension to our already fragile relationship. This was my husband, and I wanted to see progress towards our goal of reconciliation. I saw little. I still had to lead the conversations in order to get answers. His reactions and responses were those of one who seemed defeated. When the discussions turned difficult or messy, he would shut down. Conversation over.

One day a couple months into our recovery, I spoke with my close friend, Dana, on the phone. I asked her at what point I should give up. Her matter-of-fact answer startled me into the realization that love doesn't depend on circumstances, not even these horrific ones.

"Well, it's hard since you love him. You go until you feel there has been no more progress. Then, you assess where you are at and decide if you can live with it."

I love him. She said it as a fact. It was. Strange as it sounds, I needed the reminder. I had been questioning my love for Marc because of the deep hurt, anger, and hopelessness I had been feeling. But, I did still love him.

I began to understand that in today's world, the idea of love has perhaps changed from what God initially intended. Maybe we have turned the idea of love into not what we give to a relationship, but what we get out of it. Love should not depend on circumstances or actions. If it did, none of us would be lovable. I realized that marriage designed by God should be filled with sacrificial love. I became willing to pray and sacrifice much in this marriage story of mine in the hopes that Marc would lean on God and sacrifice too. Marc may have broken his vows, but that did not mean I should break mine.

Finally, I asked Marc if he would return to our bed. My reasoning went something like this: I needed some boundaries and separation while I was at the bottom of my emotional tank. Alone time was what I had craved during those first several weeks. However, now that we were working so hard to mend our broken marriage, I wanted to reach out with an act of peace too. I wanted my husband to know that I was not going to just give up. I had resolved to work at this. We both knew, however, that it was going to take a miracle from God in order for our marriage to succeed. In the waiting, I prayed for that miracle. We slept as far apart as we could in our queen size bed.

I also set up some non-negotiable rules to protect my heart, my children, and our home. If he acted out through his addictive behavior, he knew I would immediately ask him to leave. Our marriage would be over. There would be no second chances. No debate. No arguments.

I knew that while I could not control the outcome or my husband's decisions—not with anger, or pleading, or love—I could lean on God in ways that would leave me always hopeful and able to find joy, regardless of the circumstances. Admitting powerlessness and kneeling before God was difficult but also gave me a sense of freedom and peace I had never known before.

"I depend on God alone; I put my hope in him. He alone protects and saves me; he is my defender, and I shall never be defeated. My salvation and honor depend on God; he is my strong protector; he is my shelter. Trust in God at all times, my people. Tell him all your troubles, for he is our refuge." (Psalm 62:5–8, in the Good News Translation)

I read 2 Corinthians 4 every day. As my support group began to challenge me with introspective honesty, I held on to a particular verse in that Scripture. I knew I had to be completely candid with myself if I was going to come out the other side of this experience fully restored.

"Therefore, since through God's mercy we have this ministry, we do not lose heart. Rather, we have renounced secret and shameful ways; we do not use deception, nor do we distort the word of God. On the contrary, by setting forth the truth plainly we commend ourselves to everyone's conscience in the sight of God." (2 Corinthians 4:1–2, in the NIV)

God wanted to get honest with me, and now I was in a position to finally listen. He wanted me to be entirely dependent on Him. While I have rarely made the mistake of fully depending on others, my downfall was a radically focused dependency on myself. My overly competitive, self-driven, and strong-minded personality fueled my ego. I lost sight of the One who had given me every talent, skill, and personality trait for which I boasted. My daily reading of 2 Corinthians 4, my new life verse, reminded me, "But we have this treasure in jars of clay to show that this all-surpassing power is from God *and not from us* (emphasis mine)."

I began to realize that perhaps while God had not caused this anguish, He had allowed it to happen because there was a development plan in play for me. God was molding my character. He was breaking me of my unhealthy self-dependency. All my egotistical dreams, ambitious plans, and fear of failures were starting to dim in light of the knowledge that trusting God is important. If I genuinely believed His plan was the best way, I had better start living my life that way.

After one ugly argument on our family room couch, I walked out the front door into the cool night air. I needed to walk around the block and settle my emotions. It was ten fifteen p.m. I remember because after the quick quarter-mile loop, I secretly entered our back gate and stood in the shadows of our back yard. Peering in through the wall of windows to our family room, I saw the clock on the mantel. I did not see Marc. I assumed he had gone to bed. I looked up into the sky and prayed, *God, I am not going to ask the "why" question. It doesn't matter. "Why me?" does nothing for me now. I am already here—in this place. So, I am going to ask, "What now?" Just tell me what you want me to do. I am yours. I know I cannot depend on myself to get through this. So, I am asking You, "What now?"*

I sensed immediately that God was going to show me the way. I felt my question was a good one, one that pleased God. I was learning that dependency on Him was all that mattered.

The Story of the Hamster Wheel:
Not "Why Me?" but "What Now?"

November 29, 2012

**"But I have raised you up for this very purpose,
that I might show you my power and that my
name might be proclaimed in all the earth."**

Exodus 9:16

I stood in the pet store and watched the hamster spinning his rickety wheel. "That's us," I thought out loud. Our lives had become one giant hamster wheel where every day we woke up, took part in the same routine tasks packaged as the "American Dream," and then went to bed feeling exhausted yet unfulfilled. My husband and I watched the hamster for a few more minutes. "Using all that energy and going nowhere," my husband observed. We went home feeling depressed.

The depressed mood came and went for several years. We knew life was more than the American Dream. It's more than jobs, grocery stores, car repairs, sick kids, karate, church, birthday parties, bills, friends, or even success. We knew God created us for a very specific purpose, and we were not living it yet. We just didn't know how to find that specific purpose!

Explaining this feeling to others was difficult. We had been small group leaders and volunteered in a myriad of opportunities inside and outside the church. Some people thought that was "enough" … but God wasn't done with us yet.

Our marriage and spirits had already survived more than three years of infertility struggles. Due to those struggles, our God-ordained path had taken us to Russia and then to China for the adoption of our children. In many cases, people thought that was "enough" … but God wasn't done with us yet.

My husband and I read the book "Radical" by David Platt. One of many thought-provoking quotes from his book is " … have we replaced what is radical about our faith with what is comfortable? Are we settling for Christianity that revolves around catering to ourselves when the central message of Christianity is actually about abandoning ourselves?" We wondered what we might abandon to be radical about discovering God's purpose for us.

Over the next few months, we continued to sense that God was preparing us for something big. I felt as if I was ready for anything—anything that would help us define our purpose. Be careful what you pray for! One day it materialized. Terrible news rocked my world. Exodus 9:16 says, "But I have raised you up for this very purpose, that I might show you my power and that my name might be proclaimed in all the earth." It's a powerfully intimidating verse if you are willing to follow it to the end of God's story and not just to the limited expectations of how you want your story to read. We were about to abandon the hamster wheel.

God had been relentlessly preparing our hearts so that when the time came, we would not fall down but be raised up for the purpose He designed for us. Queen Esther knew a little something about being raised up to fulfill a God-given destiny. In Esther 4:14, as she is learning about the plans to murder all the Jewish people such as herself, it reads, "And who knows but that you have come to your royal position for such a time as this?" When our world fell apart, most people would have run for the hills—we fell to our knees. From our "royal" position, we asked, "What now, God?" instead of asking, "Why me, God?"

See, the "Why us?" question had been answered throughout all the years following the visit to that pet store. We abandoned the "Why us?" because the answer is it's ALL of us. All of us will go through a crisis. All of us will make choices about how we respond to those crises. All of us have weaknesses that are made perfect through Christ who strengthens us. All of us have a destiny. So, when the time came for our specific destiny to be revealed, the better question became, "What now, God? What do we do now? Show us how You will make this beautiful. Help us understand what we can do to use this for your story for us—a story that will glorify You and impact many if we choose to say yes."

Do you sometimes feel like you are running on that hamster wheel? Do you get to the end of a day and ask, "What is the point?" Do you sense a bigger purpose for your life? My guess is that it's a common feeling … to believe God has a plan for you that is more significant than any "American Dream." When tough times come, perhaps you will choose to change your question. Rather than asking God, "Why me?" try asking Him, "What now?" You might just get an answer that will bump you off that rickety wheel and change your life forever!

Character-Building Class was in session. God was the teacher: I, the student. My self-dependency and misguided marriage had manifested into a separation between God and me as I elevated someone else ahead of God in my life—Marc. I had effectively closed off the most significant benefits of what a relationship with a Heavenly Father and Wonderful Counselor can produce.

Throughout our marriage, when trouble found me, I sought out Marc's advice first. When difficult days came, I ran after Marc and expected him to give me all the encouragement I needed. As we walked through challenges in our lives, big and small, Marc and I had traditionally banded together as a team of two, leaving God outside our own intimate circle.

So, while Marc was struggling with his past and his demons, God had me focusing on my relationship with Him. I reordered my priorities. I prayed daily, sometimes hourly, to communicate authentically with the only One who could sustain me.

All this God work inside me caused a transformation. With God's help, I decided not to become a bitter, frightened, and paranoid wife, always ready for bad news with every breath of conversation. Instead, I began to hear the sarcasm I was using, and slowly, I learned how to rephrase my words to change their intent. Accusations such as, "You don't even know me" turned into offerings like, "Let me tell you what I am feeling and thinking." Rather than immediately blaming Marc for not initiating conversations, I paused long enough for him to gather his thoughts and begin to share.

Then, an amazing thing happened. Marc began to transform too. He initiated some of the late night conversations. He started going deeper, sharing feelings and thoughts and not simply reactions and explanations. As the months went by, it seemed he was gaining clarity and confidence in both his recovery and our relationship. As spring neared, my hope grew. One day, I caught us laughing and joking together for the first time in many months.

God had molded my character through this long recovery. I had become a strong and accountable spouse with a growing ability to forgive. I also accepted the responsibility that comes with being in relationships. Yes, Marc betrayed and abandoned me. Yes, it was a pain like nothing else. But, Jesus bore the wounds and scars on that cross that would forgive and cleanse me of my own sins. To refuse to forgive everyone involved in this messy story would have said to Jesus that what He gave me was not enough. I could not do that. We are more than our wounds. We are the recipients of the gift of Christ's wounds. I vowed to work on that process of forgiveness. After all, there was a long list of people I knew I had to forgive.

Chapter 7
INDEPENDENCE DAY

Forgiveness is part of the substance holding my fragile jar together. It's the mending of the vast chasm between God and me, the crack glued together by Christ's work. Jesus taught me how to forgive.

For this story, forgiveness was simply my intentional act of handing over my raging anger, bitterness, and resentment to God so that I could be free of the weight of the pain and from Satan's stronghold. It was, in essence, freedom. It did not cover up responsibility or even feelings. I still have feelings. The feelings related to my story won't ever leave me.

"God, you know I don't want to say this. I certainly don't believe it yet. I will say the words out loud, but You, Father God, will need to help me get to the place of meaning it. God, I forgive these women. They knew Marc was married—each and every one of them. I want to hate them. I know that hatred is wrong—a feeling that would keep me from you. I am in a battle. These women stole so much from me. I will not let them steal my eternity with You, too. So, I will say I forgive them, but really I don't. Of course, You know that already. I need Your help to get there."

This is the outline of the prayer I said every morning for four months. Then, one day it happened. I ended my morning prayer and knew in my heart that I had forgiven these women of the unthinkable. I was able to say, "God, I know you are the God of justice, and this is not my battle to fight. I forgive them because I do not want to carry around that kind of hatred. It's a weight I am lifting up to You because only You can handle it. I forgive them. I no longer need revenge. That baggage is too heavy for me to carry. They are not holding me back anymore. Now, I pray for them, Lord. I pray they come to know You on an intimate level, one that will force them to stop and assess their own lives and choices. I pray for their families. In Jesus' name … Amen."

That day, I meant it.

From that point forward, I gave little thought to the other women. It was nice. I had never realized what grudges and hatred can do to a person's soul. Mine felt much lighter.

My ability to forgive Marc would come later. I continued to ask God to help me genuinely feel what my prayers verbally conveyed. For way too many months, I had been furious about what Marc had taken from our marriage. Trust. Honesty. Respect. Intimacy. It was difficult to imagine forgiving him for his poor choices.

While our kids had not learned about his addiction, they had certainly felt the tension in our home. They saw me leaving on Wednesday evenings for weeks and had received no clear answer about where I was going. I'm sure they had sensed the lack of respect I had for their dad. They had watched us move through this dark season at a distance from each other, simply going through the motions of our daily routines.

Thankfully, God sets His miracles in the cracks of our broken jars. Liz Curtis Higgs, a fabulously anointed writer and speaker, once said, "God loves to work in the realm of the impossible because He gets all the glory." God was about to unleash another miracle.

A few days before Independence Day, while our nation was busy planning to celebrate the freedoms we all cherish, God reached out to give me a spiritually eternal freedom that would prove even more priceless. I was alone in my car, singing along to my favorite music. As I traveled down a small town road, I sensed the now familiar voice of God whisper, "Now." I knew in an instant what He meant. After all, we had been having this conversation for a long time. It was time to forgive Marc. It had been almost eleven months since that first horrific disclosure. God was about to answer my empty but intentional prayers. I was about to forgive the unforgivable … and it would be oh-so-good.

On July 4th, I sat down and explained to Marc that I no longer felt that he owed me anything. I harbored no animosity or malice. My white-hot anger of so many months was gone. I still felt sad. I remained cautious. The forgiveness was not erasing the hurt and pain; they were still there. But, I no longer felt the need to hate, to exact revenge, to hold him in contempt, or to seek repayment for all I had lost. I had given all that over to Christ.

I explained to Marc that I believed without forgiveness, the death of Jesus on the cross would be in vain. Colossians 3:13 in the NIV says, "Bear with each other and forgive one another if any of you has a grievance against someone. Forgive as the Lord forgave you." If I wanted to follow the Lord, and if I strived every day to be more like Christ, I knew forgiving my husband would be part of that hard faith walk. My earlier unforgiveness had prevented me from completely grasping God's goodness and preventing Marc from receiving His forgiveness. "If you forgive anyone's sins, their sins are forgiven; if you do not forgive them, they are not forgiven." (John 20:23) Marc sat in stunned silence. I smiled. I was finally free.

My freedom from those negative feelings and thoughts and the bondage they created was a major milestone. However, there were two other milestones I had to overcome in this long (and becoming longer) process.

Trust. As an echo of my friends' questions, I asked myself regularly, *How will I ever trust my husband again?* I didn't think we could have much of a marriage without full trust. I spent hours praying about this particular crack in our marriage jar.

The answer to my question came over time. I discovered it was a much simpler answer than I had anticipated. I don't trust Marc. And, it's okay. I probably never will trust him wholly. I realize this may seem somewhat sad and pessimistic if taken at face value. Bear with me and consider …

Blind and unearned trust had been one of the mistakes I had made in our "old marriage." I had looked at Marc and seen a man who could do no wrong. I viewed my husband as perfect—as someone who was not even capable of such betrayal. The truth is we all are capable. Given the right circumstances, the wrong choices, the temptations that snake through our private worlds, and the freedom to live apart from God if we choose to do so, we will all make mistakes. Sometimes they will be life changing, heart-stomping, guilt-producing mistakes. We are human.

I don't trust Marc (or anyone else) one hundred percent. I certainly don't trust myself to avoid every sin-filled pitfall. I will never be perfect. Some may call this perspective dysfunctional or down-right negative. I disagree. I prefer to think I have grown out of my naivety.

I don't trust any person fully, but I do trust God. I trust Him completely. People will hurt me. It's happened all my life. The hurt has been intentional, unintentional, direct, and indirect. I will continue to face rejection, abandonment, pain, anguish, selfishness, and pride. Those cracks will continue to scratch my clay jar as long as I enter into relationships. Yet, God will stand by me and hold me through it all. I know this because He has proven it time after time. In her book *One Thousand Gifts,* Ann Voskamp writes, "Thank God for the past and you can trust him for the future. Trust is a bridge from past to future built with planks of thanks."

God had pulled me out of this addiction ravine for months. He had supplied me with hiding places, genuine friends to lean on, hope and love that covered my wounds, and I saw the good that was blossoming from the tragedy. My fragile clay jar was still whole—cracked but not shattered. His promises never failed. I can trust God.

When I look up to God instead of out to my husband for that kind of peace and foundational support, I am defined as a daughter of The Almighty and not a broken bride of a sinful man. When I look up, I am not dependent on any flesh and blood but on the Maker of the Heavens. I have learned what it means to put God first and husband second.

In fact, understanding this relationship hierarchy is what has allowed me to trust Marc as much as I do—we are both in God's hands. People must earn our trust. No matter what happens in the future, I will be okay. As I pray for continued intimacy and sobriety within our marriage, I know that God is there. He will hold me through the ups and downs, carry me over the hurdles, and cover me with His hand when I find myself in any cleft—just as He did this time. Ann Voskamp also writes, "If trust must be earned, hasn't God unequivocally earned our trust with the bark on the raw wounds, the thorns pressed into the brow, your name on the cracked lips." I think so.

When I put that kind of faith in the God who sacrificed His Son, and not in any other individual, there is a certain level of peace that absolutely transcends my narrowly focused understanding. It is not up to me to control or enforce anything within our marriage. It is not up to me to ensure there are no more lies, no more secrets, and no more betrayals. It is up to Marc to do the right thing and stay close to God. I will not be a wife who clings to her husband, hoping he makes the right choices out of fear for my own life's story—for fear of more cracks in my jar. I cling to God, the one who is writing my story and making it good. I trust God because He has earned it when no one else has come close.

As months passed and I saw Marc's commitment to sobriety, restoration, and rebuilding our marriage, I started to breathe easier. I began to loosen my grip and my need to control all our communication. Thorough details from his sessions with his counselor were still important to me, but I no longer needed to hear them within a couple of hours of his return home. One day, I told him I no longer needed to have his mobile phone in plain view.

As forgiveness (freedom) came and I built trust with God, the third milestone on my journey through this trial was revealed: Finding joy.

Just One Word

Jan 1, 2013

"You love righteousness and hate wickedness; therefore God, your God, has set you above your companions by anointing you with the oil of joy."

Psalm 45:7

Words are powerful.

Last year I started a new tradition. Rather than struggling to keep a New Year's Resolution through three hundred sixty-five days of pure torture, I opted to live by a "Word of the Year." This word would guide my decisions, my thoughts, my actions, and even my reactions. My word for 2012 was "PEACE." An unknown individual once made this statement: "Peace. It does not mean to be in a place where there is no noise, trouble or hard work; it means to be in the midst of those things and still be calm in your heart." I invite you to take a step back with me into my year of Peace …

The past eighteen months started off hard. There really is no other word to describe it. There were countless people who had stepped all over my heart strings, and I was struggling to forgive them. There was leftover chaos from moving my son to a new school and rebuilding his confidence and self-esteem. Our kids were yelling at each other on an hourly basis. We were engaged in too many activities, creating an atmosphere of endless running. My house was a mess. My husband and I were "two ships passing in the night" as we tag-teamed taxi services for after-school activities and attended our own evening meetings. Friends—whom I don't know what I would do without—watched our children many evenings as we continued this crazy schedule. On January 1st, I said, "enough."

I adopted the idea of living with the peace of Christ in order to end the family chaos and move on with the forgiveness that eluded me. This peace was never going to be something I could accomplish alone. God was going to be an integral part of this new plan for our family. For the next twelve months, with every decision my husband and I made, we asked ourselves, "Will this bring peace or more chaos to our home?" We learned to say "no" to activities, groups, and meetings that were not critical to our lives. Our son participated in only one after school activity at a time, and our preschool-aged daughter could choose one outside hobby as well. Slowly our lives slowed down enough to breath.

I sat with God every day and prayed about forgiveness. I knew the bitterness, resentment, anger, and hurt that were housed in my *heart were soaking through my pores, affecting my attitude and stealing my joy. The unforgiveness was hurting me more than those who had wronged me. My prayers for God's grace and mercy to take over residence in my heart became constant. I knew I had to grab hold of that peace that surpasses the flesh's understanding—Christ's Peace—and hold on tight.*

On July 4th, I finally accomplished one of the hardest things for many people to do—I forgave the unforgivable. That Independence Day, I was no longer dependent on anger or resentment. I did not do it alone. God walked me through every step of the process. He did so because I was actively choosing peace rather than revenge and bitterness. In October, a family member who did not know about our "Word of the Year" initiative shared these sentiments with us during a visit: "Your house is so much more peaceful than mine. It's quiet. It's nice." My heart beamed. With God, all things are possible!

This brings me to the New Year—2013.

*Proverbs 12:20 says, "Deceit is in the hearts of those who plot evil, but those who promote **peace** have **joy**."*

I prayed for a few weeks about which word to choose for 2013. The word "JOY" kept coming to me, but I fought it. It seemed too simple, too cliché. Yet time and time again, God pressed in on me. I sensed He wanted me to have the gift of joy in return for my obedience. One day, God showed me Psalm 45:7, and it all made sense. The work I had done towards removing chaos, slowing down to be with God, creating peace in our home, and forgiving others was going to lead to something really awesome. **"You love righteousness and hate wickedness; therefore God, your God, has set you above your companions by anointing you with the oil of JOY."**

I am looking forward with great anticipation to my year of joy! Just as with my year of peace, I envision the joy will come from my specific and very intentional decisions and actions, ones that will be continually focused on Christ. For example, I am not so naïve to think that living in a year filled with joy will not come with challenges or even sadness. I do not think it means every day will be filled with happiness or that I am responsible for others' happiness. I anticipate my anointing of joy will show itself in my gratitude for what I do have … for those things for which God has blessed to me. No matter what circumstances I find myself in, I can—and will—choose joy and thanksgiving. That is my promise to myself this year.

How about you? Can I challenge you to pray about a word for your life in 2013? I know God will have something incredible in store for you! By God's design and not my own, my words have come from the fruit of the Spirit. Perhaps yours will too?

Galatians 5:22 "But the fruit of the Spirit is love, joy, peace, patience, kindness, goodness, faithfulness"

The peace gained through forgiveness and the hope secured by trusting God preceded this joy. As Marc and I started to laugh together again, as we prayed together, and as we leaned on Jesus together, our marriage started to heal. We began to heal.

Over the next few months, I began to not just see but experience how God was making this all good. Our marriage was feeling stronger than it ever had. Our conversations were authentic and deep. Our relationships with God had grown immeasurably. I even began to ask myself the craziest question: *Could all this be worth it?*

Chapter 8
WORTH IT

*"I have told you these things so that you may have peace.
In this world you will have trouble, but take heart! I have
overcome the world."*
— Jesus Christ (John 13:33, paraphrased)

Once the pain subsided and our lives were restored with joy, there was one overarching question I spent a lot of time considering: *Does someone have to experience something tragic to truly understand what it means to follow Jesus?* In other words, does something horrific always precede the all-out surrender to God? Do we have to hit rock bottom to really "get it" and be willing to give up everything for Jesus?

Before Marc's double life was brought to light, I would have proclaimed that I was a true Christ follower. I had prayed "the prayer," been baptized, volunteered my time, sacrificed my money to the church in the form of a tithe, and engaged in (albeit sporadic) quiet times reading my Bible. My husband and I had even led a small group within our church, and I desperately wanted my children to know Jesus on an intimate level. The truth was I didn't know Jesus intimately. My prayer life was stale. I was still putting my dreams ahead of God's will and plans for me. My faith was a rollercoaster ride—all too dependent on the circumstances of my life.

I would have been better classified as a Jesus "fan." Kyle Idleman, author of *Not a Fan*, keenly writes, "In part, this is due to the collision of Christianity with American capitalism. It has created a culture of consumers in our churches. Instead of approaching their faith with a spirit of denial that says, 'What can I do for Jesus?' they have a consumer mentality that says, 'What can Jesus do for me?'" Unfortunately, that second question was the groundwork of my relationship with my Savior prior to this marriage mess of ours. *What can Jesus do for me?* Most times, my own hopes and dreams filled my prayers. I prayed about how God might help me reach my goals in life rather than concentrating on what God had in store for me and what grand plan He had in mind when He knit me together.

I justified greed by calling it ambition. I rationalized pride and called it self-confidence. My focus was earthly success, getting ahead of our financial plateau, living a safe and "good" life, while ensuring my kids had everything Marc and I could provide that would classify us as successful parents. My misguided faith was clear in my prayers. *God, please help me (fill in the blank) ... Amen.* That was it. I was missing the dangerously radical commitment to—and adventure with—Jesus that can only come through a deep relationship with Him and through total submission to His will. Until my clay jar cracked up and down with Marc's admissions, I was nowhere near dying to myself daily ... not even annually. My eyes and heart had been closed off to Jesus's message in Matthew 8:34—38 (in the NIV):

"Then he called the crowd to him along with his disciples and said, 'Whoever wants to be my disciple must deny themselves and take up their cross and follow me. For whoever wants to save their life will lose it, but whoever loses their life for me and for the gospel will save it. What good is it for someone to gain the whole world, yet forfeit their soul? Or what can anyone give in exchange for their soul? If anyone is ashamed of me and my words in this adulterous and sinful generation, the Son of Man will be ashamed of them when he comes in his Father's glory with the holy angels."

For years, I had been trying to gain the world—a world with all its faults, self-indulgence, comparison games, and idols. Even the name of Jesus was sometimes awkward for me to say out loud. I was forfeiting my soul.

Audience of One

Sept 3, 2013

"Do not conform to the pattern of this world, but be transformed by the renewing of your mind. Then you will be able to test and approve what God's will is — his good, pleasing, and perfect will."

Romans 12:2

This is hard work—the work of renewing my mind.

In this society, we, the heirs of Christ's labor, are met with the same temptations, rejection, and loneliness that Jesus Himself experienced before nearly everyone in Jerusalem convinced a hesitant Pilate to crucify Him. Yet, all that did not stop Jesus from approving God's will. In Matthew 26:39, Jesus prays, " …My Father, if it is possible, may this cup be taken from me. Yet not as I will, but as you will." *Even though He knew death was coming, Jesus lived for an audience of One.*

The first obstacle in renewing my mind is my wanting so badly to conform to this world. The temptation I fall prey to time after time is the comparison temptation. I will be honest and tell you that sometimes I look at others and wonder how they do it. The it is any area where I feel as if I am losing in that silly comparison game. How do they … buy the new car, build the new deck, manage three kids in different activities, work full-time, exercise five days a week, get the promotion, walk the dog regularly, save more money … you name it, *I have compared* it. *The pattern of this world seems to be this: acquire a good education, secure a high-paying job, grow a happy and well-rounded family, send said children to elite colleges and universities, and retire early as the next generation accepts your high-paying job.*

I have to ask myself why? *Is the answer because that is what others are doing? Is that a good enough answer? Are people finding joy in this pattern? Am I?*

The second dilemma I face in renewing my mind is where I place my focus. I grew up looking for others' approval, whether it was my parents, teachers, coaches, or friends. After awhile, I learned to set my own lofty expectations, ones that always seemed focus on success. Until my mid-thirties, my goals were aligned with the patterns of this world: graduate with a master's degree, secure a high-paying job, start a family of mini-mees, raise them "right," and retire "happy." I found little joy living with this focus. I lived with the feeling that something was missing. Actually, it was more than that—I felt I was not doing what I was created to do. In my innermost parts, I knew that life had to be more than this simple-minded pattern that propels all of us toward the grave. I wanted a life filled with joy that propelled me to an eternity in the Hands of my Father.

In my mid-thirties, God poked my heart hard enough for me to truly understand what it meant to surrender all—surrender the pattern of this world—the one that was fast-tracking me to a life of loneliness, stress, and selfishness. God was beginning to transform me. Rather than a legacy of success, I suddenly wanted to leave a legacy of living in God's will. My past audience of parents, employers, friends, and neighbors dwindled down to just an audience of one—God. You know what happened?

The comparison game ended. My focus changed. Joy sprung up from within. My purpose was clear. My legacy was forever altered. My mind continues to be renewed.

The founder of Campus Crusade for Christ, Bill Bright, has this on his gravestone: "Slave for Jesus." Now that is a powerful legacy to leave. You can't get more in tune with God's will and perfect plan than living as a slave for Jesus. It helped Bill Bright not only found a national ministry affecting millions for God, but he also played an integral role in the production of the Jesus film in 1979. According to The New York Times, *Jesus is likely the most-watched motion picture of all time. The Jesus Film Project states that Jesus has been viewed more than six billion times (including repeat viewings).*

That is what I want. I want to live for an audience of One. I want to talk, act, think, pray, serve, eat, work, volunteer, raise my kids, and live my one and only life for something bigger than any earthly accomplishment. My successes will die when I do. I want my legacy for Christ to live forever as purpose-driven and joyful change that was brought about while doing life for God and impacting others for His Kingdom. Maybe you want that too?

I never imagined what carrying a cross really meant. According to Jesus as recorded in Luke 14:27, "…whoever does not carry their cross and follow me cannot be my disciple." As further explanation of Jesus's message from these Scriptures, Matthew Henry's Whole Bible Commentary states, "He is in these verses directing his discourse to the multitudes that crowded after him, and seemed zealous in following him; and his exhortation to them is to understand the terms of discipleship, before they undertook the profession of it, and to consider what they did."

Jesus knows the seriousness of the commitment to follow Him. He knows what we will sacrifice and how hard it can be to surrender all. Truthfully, I think many of us do too. It's why I may have failed to fully surrender for so long. I knew it would take work and courage to be all-in for God's purpose and will for my life. It takes a certain understanding of the incentives versus the consequences—earthly versus eternal—to make the decision to take up our crosses and die every single day. There is an inherent risk.

You Gotta Play to Win
October 1, 2013

"The time came when the beggar (Lazarus) died and the angels carried him to Abraham's side. The rich man also died and was buried. In Hades, where he was in torment, he looked up and saw Abraham far away, with Lazarus by his side."

Luke 16:22–23

I have certain boundaries that I like to believe keep me safe.

I refuse to leave the house with the clothes dryer running, I don't play with fire or run with scissors, and I always avoid shiny plants with three leaves. This helps me to avoid burned houses, lost eyesight, and itchy rashes. Likewise, I don't typically play the lottery. It's too risky. Gambling addiction is not something to which I want to fall prey. Only if the jackpot is $33 million, $333 million, or more than $500 million, will I buy a ticket. I set boundaries for myself when it comes to taking risks. It's just what I do.

So, when my husband sent me a text saying his co-workers were going in together on the $600 million Powerball lottery, my response was simple: "You gotta play to win." As I hit send on my return text, the phrase rang a bell in my heart. I know the sound well. God was giving me another title.

Soon, a question took up residence inside me: Why don't more people accept Jesus' invitation to follow Him? *I think many of us would answer:* Because it's risky.

There is a risk in going all-in with God. Maybe we believe that we will miss out on certain things if we become truly committed to His will—comfort, happiness, security, wealth, our own plan for our lives, relationships … the list goes on. The truth is there is a risk.

But I have to share something: In the "following Jesus" gamble of a lifetime, both the reward AND the journey itself are worth the risk! If we are not able to surrender those earthly things we tend to over-value, we may lose what God values for our eternity. In fact, at the end of our lives, whether we win or lose in God's eyes is the only thing that matters. The rich man in the story of Luke 16 was successful by society's standards. The fear of losing everything of value if He chose to follow God outweighed his understanding of what he might gain for his sacrifice. He believed the risk too great. He chose his worldly possessions over a God who could give him everything he would ever need for thousands of years to come. This rich man didn't play to win; he played to lose. And he lost big!

Luke shares a story told by Jesus to help illustrate the enormity of not playing to win for God's glory. Jesus wanted the message to be clear: The risk is worth the reward. **"The time came when the beggar died and the angels carried him to Abraham's side. The rich man also died and was buried. In Hades, where he was in torment, he looked up and saw Abraham far away, with Lazarus by his side."** *Our lives here are temporary. Possessions, success, material goods and accolades—they all stay here when we leave this earth. If we choose Jesus now, our illnesses, our fears, our pain and our tears will vanish when we meet Jesus in Heaven.*

In his book, "Not a Fan," Kyle Idleman writes, "The most dangerous part of following Jesus tomorrow isn't what you will lose between now and then. That's not the worst thing that can happen. The worst thing that can happen is that tomorrow might never come." *We are not promised another day here in our temporary home. One day, tomorrow never came for the rich man in the Book of Luke. He lost based on his choices on earth. Once he realized that, he tried to save his brothers who were living much like he had.*

"*So he (the rich man)* called to him, 'Father Abraham, have pity on me and send Lazarus to dip the tip of his finger in water and cool my tongue, because I am in agony in this fire.'

But Abraham replied, 'Son, remember that in your lifetime you received your good things, while Lazarus received bad things, but now he is comforted here and you are in agony. And besides all this, between us and you a great chasm has been set in place, so that those who want to go from here to you cannot, nor can anyone cross over from there to us.'

He answered, 'Then I beg you, father, send Lazarus to my family, for I have five brothers. Let him warn them, so that they will not also come to this place of torment.'

Abraham replied, 'They have Moses and the Prophets; let them listen to them.'

'No, father Abraham,' he said, 'but if someone from the dead goes to them, they will repent.'

He said to him, 'If they do not listen to Moses and the Prophets, they will not be convinced even if someone rises from the dead.'"

For me, this story is quite frightening. It paints a scary picture of Hades and calls it a "place of torment"—as in a forever and ever *place of torment.*

The Bible makes this plain and simple: There is one guaranteed way to heaven—through a decision for Christ made now. Not tomorrow. Not next year. Not when the kids are grown. Not when you retire. Certainly not when you have your life together. Jesus died on that cross and rose from the dead for you—for me—for now. You gotta play to win today.

Tomorrow just may be too late.

Oh—and the Powerball lottery outcome? We won! Eight dollars split eight ways. Kaboom!

So, how did I move from being a fan of Jesus to becoming a completely surrendered servant for His mission and cause? My cozy and safe world was ripped out from underneath me. My fragile jar was exposed. I learned I was the spouse of a sex addict. And, I thank God for it every day.

When my daily focus changed and narrowed from *how can I be successful in this world* to *how can I survive the next hour,* God grew. He grew so immense that the only place I could find rest for my broken heart was to envision myself lying in the fetal position, in the dark spaces beneath his massive wings. Under those wings, I met Jesus and found His loving mercy. Instantly, Jesus was all I had left.

I had my children to care for, and I had work responsibilities I had to carry out to keep my job. I was on autopilot for those responsibilities. I loved my children, and I shielded them from the pain and truth. Yet, the best thing I did for them during that time was pray for them and slip under those feathered wings to make sure I could heal. Without healing, I knew my children would not have the mother they deserved. So, my focus shifted to Jesus, the Ultimate Healer.

Guess what else I found under those wings? I found truth. *Marc's affairs were not your fault.* I found peace. *Trust me. You won't shatter. I will make this good.* I found my purpose. *Will you use this to serve others in My name?* I found encouragement that went far beyond kind words and hugs from friends. I found the cross and every good and perfect meaning behind it. I became a servant—no, a slave. Jesus became Lord of Lords in every sense and meaning. In *Mere Christianity*, C.S. Lewis declares, "Christ says, 'Give me all. I don't want so much of your time and so much of your money and so much of your work: I want you. I have not come to torment your natural self, but to kill it. No half-measures are any good." I felt killed, and it was so good!

I started to pray harder. Mark Batterson, author of *The Circle Maker*, writes, "Praying hard is going twelve rounds with God … Praying hard is more than words; it's blood, sweat, and tears." I bled. Sweat poured. I definitely shed some tears during this journey. I felt God open up opportunities that I never would have anticipated. I learned what it meant to have a holy desperation. It seemed God and I interacted daily on a newly intimate level.

I began to find a purpose that went far beyond salaries, status, possessions, and power. My spirit, that inner strength that comes from God, was energized. I was scared but excited about what I felt God was showing me about how to live a godly life.

In the book The Lion, the Witch, and the Wardrobe by C.S. Lewis, there is an exchange between Lucy, one of the main characters who finds the portal to Narnia, and Mr. Beaver, a good-humored character who lives in Narnia. They are talking about the Lion (aka God).

"Then he isn't safe?" said Lucy.

"Safe?" said Mr. Beaver. "Don't you hear what Mrs. Beaver tells you? Who said anything about being safe? 'Course he isn't safe. But he's good ..."

There are many moments of my story that have been etched like tattoos into my memory and onto my jar. Moments that if I sit still with for a period of time, will cause me to once again feel the hurt, experience the gut-wrenching pain, and release the emotions of sorrow and anguish related to Marc's betrayal. Lying on my bathroom floor and feeling God's promise that He would make all this good is one of them.

In that one tick of the clock, just as with the tick of the clock that Marc's admission of extramarital sex brought me to my knees, I knew in my deepest parts that I was fully surrendering to God and would do whatever He asked in order to make sure there was a good ending to this tragic story. God's good ending, not mine.

I was learning that this marriage story would end in redemption and perhaps more importantly, in service to others. God impressed upon my clay jar that there would be opportunity to not only make this good, but to make it great. God would restore this dark, awful crack in my fragile jar.

But, that wasn't all. Then, His light would shine out through my obedience in moving my story forward. I knew in that instant, curled up on that hard floor, that I would share my story with thousands. I didn't know how I would get there, and I certainly did not know what kind of ending I would be telling. That was okay.

No, God is not safe. Following God is not safe. It's radical. It will cause you to feel unsure of yourself. Others may recoil at the idea or never understand the significance of your choices or actions. Most will only watch you from a distance, never jumping in with you. It is risky. It is worth it.

Jesus wants all of me. It took falling to my knees in utter anguish to discover all that Jesus offers to each and every one of us. It took the implosion of my family and home to find what Jesus was after all along—the recognition of my own need for a Savior that can change my life and bring me into eternity to sit at a table in the Kingdom Mansion. His is a love that can conquer all pain, all fear, all sorrow, all brokenness, all darkness, every addiction, every crime, every evil act, every orphan's despair, every widow's nightmare, and every poverty-stricken plight on the face of the earth. That is one powerful love.

I do not believe my eyes would have been opened to my lack of intimacy with God had I not experienced this specific tragedy. I believe with everything inside me that if any other catastrophe had occurred, Marc and I would have pulled together to fight through it as a team ... a team that was not led by Jesus. Had our home been devastated with a horrific diagnosis or financial ruin, I fear that we were too lost in our own prideful ambitions to solve problems without looking to

Jesus first; I do not think we would have bent our souls and knees to trust God with everything. It took this nightmare, a serial crack in intimacy that split this husband and wife apart, for us to finally find Jesus on our own so that we could lift Him up as the head of our marriage too.

As I pondered this question of whether people have to hit bottom to fully surrender to Jesus, the Holy Spirit brought me back to Scripture. I thought about the most committed people in the Bible and researched their histories, their relationships with God, and the timing of their full all-in promise to live for Him—not just when they became Christians by name or baptism, but when they picked up their crosses and died to their own desires and "got it."

Throughout the three years when Jesus was teaching and performing miracles, the disciples were a primary target audience of His messages, often more so than the crowds that went to hear Him and the Pharisees that were there to discredit Him. Unfortunately, like I often do, the disciples sometimes missed Jesus' message to them:

Jesus Calms the Storm (Mark 4: 35–41, in the NIV)
That day when evening came, he said to his disciples, "Let us go over to the other side." Leaving the crowd behind, they took him along, just as he was, in the boat. There were also other boats with him. A furious squall came up, and the waves broke over the boat, so that it was nearly swamped. Jesus was in the stern, sleeping on a cushion. The disciples woke him and said to him,

"Teacher, don't you care if we drown?"

> *He got up, rebuked the wind and said to the waves,*
> *"Quiet! Be still!" Then the wind died down and it was*
> *completely calm.*
>
> *He said to his disciples, "Why are you so afraid? Do*
> *you still have no faith?"*
>
> *They were terrified and asked each other, "Who is*
> *this? Even the wind and the waves obey him!"*

By all accounts, the disciples had given up their families, their jobs, and their entire way of life to follow Jesus. They had accepted Him as their teacher and obeyed Him as their Rabbi. Yet, they still feared for their lives during the storm. I can imagine at this point in their minds, they must have been thinking *is this worth it?* I can't help but wonder if the all-in complete trust and surrender to God was missing. They were willing to sacrifice their livelihoods, but not their very lives.

In contrast, in the book of Acts after Jesus's return to Heaven, the disciples were risking their lives on a daily basis. In fact, most of them lost their lives while pursuing Jesus's last commandment—the Great Commission.

> "Then Jesus came to them and said, 'All authority
> in heaven and on earth has been given to me.
> Therefore go and make disciples of all nations,
> baptizing them in the name of the Father and of the
> Son and of the <u>Holy Spirit</u>, and teaching them to
> obey everything I have commanded you. And surely
> I am with you always, to the very end of the age."
> (Matthew 28:18–20, in the NIV)

According to Christian history, Peter was crucified in Rome under Emperor Nero Augustus Caesar. It is traditionally believed that he was crucified upside down at his own request since he saw himself unworthy to be crucified in the same way as Jesus. James was apparently beheaded. Bartholomew's fate was worse. He was skinned and then beheaded. Jude and Simon were either crucified or hacked to death. It seems no one is sure.

So, what happened in between Jesus's life and teachings and His return to Heaven after His resurrection? What was the difference that caused these men to fear a storm and then to later hang upside down or be cut to pieces for Jesus's sake? I believe it was because the disciples had experienced rock bottom.

I try to imagine living through the death of a spouse at the young age of thirty-three, when memories of the wedding itself are still fresh. Then, I imagine one of my children losing his or her favorite teacher to a tragic and sudden crime. The pain and scars those experiences would leave are huge. Next, I imagine watching a hero who had previously saved my life perish in front of my eyes while there is nothing I can do to stop it. Lastly, I imagine what it would feel like to lose my best friend, the one who knows all my secrets and celebrates all my victories with me. Devastating.

I go further. Now, I imagine what it would be like to lose all those people in the same instant. That is what the disciples experienced with Jesus's death. He was their—He is our—lover, teacher, savior, and best friend. Talk about hitting rock bottom. The anguish, the heart-pain these men and women must have felt during His crucifixion was enormous. In their minds—in their experience—death was final. Yes, Jesus had tried to tell them otherwise, but their human brains could not fathom what He was prophesying.

With no one else to turn to and nowhere else to go, the disciples stayed in Jerusalem, heart-broken and most likely paralyzed by fear. *"What do we do now?"* must have been the question that wore heavy on their minds. So, what happened? What happens when any of us hit bottom?

Jesus comes …

Jesus Appears to the Disciples (Luke 24:36–45)

While they were still talking about this (what do we do now?), *Jesus himself stood among them and said to them,* "Peace be with you."

They were startled and frightened, thinking they saw a ghost. He said to them, "Why are you troubled, and why do doubts rise in your minds? Look at my hands and my feet. It is I myself! Touch me and see; a ghost does not have flesh and bones, as you see I have."

When he had said this, he showed them his hands and feet. And while they still did not believe it because of joy and amazement, he asked them, "Do you have anything here to eat?" (At this point, they must have thought they had lost their minds.) *They gave him a piece of broiled fish, and he took it and ate it in their presence.*

He said to them, "This is what I told you while I was still with you: Everything must be fulfilled that is written about me in the Law of Moses, the Prophets and the Psalms." (Jesus is still trying to convince them.)

<u>Then</u> he opened their minds so they could understand the Scriptures (emphasis mine).

Then they were willing to sacrifice everything—their very lives even—to bring His message to all the nations and live fully abandoned. With the Holy Spirit as their guide and counselor, these men and women established the church. It became their divine purpose—their mission. Now, God has given me my mission.

Chapter 9
MISSION

"Therefore, since through God's mercy, we have this ministry, we do not lose heart."
—2 Corinthians 4:1

Marc and I both sensed God pushing us toward His purpose—to share our story. We started talking about what that might look like. We brainstormed writing books or speaking to married couples within our church or if we should target other groups. We prayed hard.

Marc had a dream one night that he had written a book. He took it as a sign and began the arduous process. I was slower to the starting line. I suppose I needed a sign too. It would come.

As my cracks mended, I felt more compelled to share my story, or at least my feelings and what I had learned. The story itself was still privy to only my close group of friends. Then, after months of prayer, Marc and I felt led to contact our church's high school ministry.

As only God can do, He impressed upon us to stand in front of a group of teenagers and share these horrific eighteen months of our lives. God can work miracles at any stage of our mistakes, but I believe He loves to be proactive. If we could reach these teens with our story before they made the same mistakes Marc and I made … if we could reach ONE teen before he or she made the same mistakes we made, it would be worth the nerves, the humiliation, and the anxiety of disclosing the story.

The evening came, and Marc and I stood in front of nearly one hundred high school students. Before we walked on stage, we prayed together. Then, we stared into each other's eyes, and said, "This is crazy." It was. But, I have learned that you don't fully live until you have followed God into the world of crazy. In his book *If,* Mark Batterson writes, "Sometimes all it takes is twenty seconds of insane courage." Not foolishness. Just courage. Our evening with the teenagers took sixty minutes. That's a lot of twenty-second increments. We were finally living outside others' expectations, outside our own expectations, outside the boundaries of the norm, and outside the gates of common sense. *Crazy.*

The teens responded with good questions, tears, grace, gratitude, and hope. Marc's and my lives were changed that night. We left the church humbled that God could take something so awful and make it so good. I felt energized and filled with joy. Finding my God-inspired purpose was exhilarating!

As a second step to sharing my story, I began writing short devotions and publishing them on a blog. It was a healing step. I felt God was writing alongside me. This particular one is my favorite.

No Scars … No Proof
March 5, 2013

"Quite frankly, I don't want to be bothered anymore by these disputes. I have far more important things to do—the serious living of this faith. I bear in my body scars from my service to Jesus."
Galatians 6:17 (The Message)

Growing up an avid athlete, I had my fair share of injuries. In fact, I had plenty of surgeries in attempts to fix those injuries, and those surgeries left a lot of scars. After my second wrist surgery to repair the torn ligaments that ended my tennis career, I had accumulated eleven scars from scalpels alone. It was then I received an amusing T-shirt from a family member. The back of the shirt read, "No scars … No proof." It reminded me that my body had taken some abuse over the years. More importantly, it reminded me of what I had received in return for those wounds—self-confidence, determination, triumph, friendship, discipline, courage, and memories that will last a lifetime. The scars were the proof of what I had gained, and they were worth it.

Jesus bore wounds that were worth our very lives. There was a disciple to whom Jesus appeared after His crucifixion—one who needed a little extra information in order to believe the Good News. In John 20:24–25, Jesus' wounds would become the proof Thomas needed of Jesus' resurrection. "One of the twelve disciples, Thomas, was not with the others when Jesus came. They told him, 'We have seen the Lord!' But he replied, 'I won't believe it unless I see the nail wounds in his hands, put my fingers into them, and place my hand into the wound in his side." *Eight days later, Jesus allowed Thomas to do just that. Those wounds were proof that the living God had come to earth, died for our sins, and rose again. Jesus was alive!*

Sometimes, our wounds are worth it too. But, our wounds are not always physical, are they? Most of us have emotional and spiritual hurts too. Thomas wasn't the only one to receive the Good News. Jesus came to heal our wounds as well—all of them. Some wounds are superficial, bleed for a short time, and are then forgiven and forgotten. Others remain active for years—similar to cuts on knuckles that keep reopening. They tear at our confidence. Jesus can heal those long-standing hurts too.

How? He stops the bleeding, and He leaves the scars. I believe if He erased our experiences and left no evidence of our pain, we might not learn from those experiences. Think about it. Would we remember them without the scars? Would we be able to turn them into powerful messages for God's gain and glory? Probably not. As they say, "Out of sight, out of mind."

Many of us try to hide our wounds and scars. I used to do this. I would cover them up, keep them private, and deny their existence. I believed they were ugly and thought if I ignored them, they would go away. Can I share something? That is a lie. As a believer, I have learned that God not only sows up our wounds and builds scars over them, but He also uses them in mighty ways—if we allow Him. Galatians 6:17 in The Message *says,* "**Quite frankly, I don't want to be bothered anymore by these disputes. I have far more important things to do—the serious living of this**

faith. I bear in my body scars from my service to Jesus." *It's time we stop being bothered by the fact that we have scars. Maybe it is time we start seeing them as God does—ugly made into beautiful. As the Scripture says, I have more important things to do than worry about what others might think—namely, I need to be living authentically for a Savior who is bigger than any wound I bear.*

All of us have wounds. It's part of life. We can stop trying to be perfect and stop pretending we are unscathed. When we allow God to heal our hurts, He does ... and leaves the scars. He doesn't erase them. Doing so would take away our memory— our message. We all carry scars that shape who we are and the decisions we make. Many times as Christ followers, we are offered the opportunity to sustain wounds and bear the scars in service to Jesus. And, what an awesome opportunity that is! After all, no scars ... no proof.

As my devotional blog took off, I began considering writing that book of so many discussions ago. However, it seemed quite overwhelming. I was terrified of failure and scared of the hard work. I was also concerned with the time it would require.

Months went by, and I continued to stall. I was hoping I could talk God out of this idea. Short devotional blog posts are one thing. Books are another. My first editor used this metaphor: Writing blog posts or devotionals are like crossing a lake. You can see the other side—the shoreline. Writing a book is like crossing an ocean. There is no shoreline to focus on. You always seem to be in the middle of it. It's hard. I continued to procrastinate.

(Not so) ironically, I had dreamed of writing a book since I had been young, probably a teenager. I had even started several books in years past, only to reach paragraph number two before realizing I had nothing significant about which to write.

I have come to learn that God had planted that writing seed in me a long time ago for this very season and purpose.

"For if you remain silent at this time, relief and deliverance for the Jews will arise from another place, but you and your father's family will perish. And who knows but that you have come to your royal position for such a time as this?" (Esther 4:14, in the NIV)

Over a year after Marc's initial disclosure, I went with my women's ministry team to a church a short distance from our home city that offered a Friday night worship experience and prophetic messages to those who wanted to receive them. I have to admit, I had my doubts. I had never experienced anything like this before. I wasn't sure I believed these people could take one look at me and get "words" or "messages" from God to give me within a few seconds time. Let me clarify: I definitely did not believe this was an authentic act of ministry. I was attending out of sheer curiosity.

After the initial time of worship, those of us on the ministry team paired off, and one of my sisters in Christ and I sat down at a round table in front of three members of this church. They were all women. I estimated them to be about our age, perhaps slightly younger. My doubts deepened. One woman stared at me for a few seconds and started writing something in a journal. I almost stood up and left. A second woman looked at me and started to speak: "Breakfast at Tiffany's.' I just keep getting 'Breakfast at Tiffany's." My friend next to me gasped. She knew my story. She had seen that movie. I had not. I had no idea what it meant. I later learned that "Breakfast at Tiffany's" is a romantic comedy about a lonely, struggling writer who becomes enchanted with his neighbor. Interesting, it was a love story.

Then, the woman at the table who had been scribbling profusely in her journal looked up at me and said, "I see a shelter. This shelter has a wall with an ivy covering. I see Jesus climbing it. You are in a season of growing. Your prospective is changing. You will see things differently. God will show you spring time … significant changes. You will be blooming. I am also getting a picture of a book. You are writing a book!" It was a proclamation, not a question.

I felt as if I could fall out of my chair. *Ok, God. Message received. Loud. And. Clear.*

Seeds
March 19, 2013
**"Light-seeds are planted in the souls of God's people,
Joy-seeds are planted in good heart-soil."**
Psalm 97:11 (The Message)

What is your seed?

I think you know what I am referring to—although you may choose to ignore the question for a host of reasons. Maybe the whisper of fear prevents you from saying it out loud. You ask, "Is God big enough?" *Perhaps anger and pain stop you from admitting you have this seed. The ugly tentacles of denial could be strangling the sound right from your voice. Or, maybe the liar is trying to convince you that you don't have what it takes—whether "it" is talent, resources, courage, time, money …*

What is your seed?

God is many things. One of His favorite occupations is planter. God plants seeds. In nature, His seeds grow into beautiful flowers, trees, vegetables, or fruits. Sometimes it happens whether others see the beauty or not—such as with wildflowers in the forest. God also plants seeds within us. Sadly, sometimes our seeds and the beauty that can grow from them are never shared either. God hopes that doesn't happen.

What is your seed?

Psalm 97:11 tells us **"Light-seeds are planted in the souls of God's people …"** *Think about that. We were created with seeds in the deepest part of our beings that have the capacity to crack open and transform into beautiful light—His light. When we were created in God's image, He planted this light-seed that shines from within, beckoning others to Him. How do I believe this works? First, let's answer the question, "What is your seed?"*

A good friend of mine once told me that she had dreamed of adopting a child when she was very young. She had even written it down as a goal in one of her school yearbooks. At age thirty-nine, that adoption seed cracked open and bloomed as she boarded an airplane for China to bring home her little girl. Now, God's light is shining through, and others are taking notice.

My husband shared with me that he had an ambition for public speaking as a child, but he never thought the opportunity was right. At age thirty-seven, that speaking seed cracked open and bloomed as he stood on a stage in front of dozens of teenagers to share an important message God had deposited within him. Now, God's light is shining through, and others are taking notice.

My light-seed was writing. For years, I attempted to put my ideas on paper without success. Then, at age thirty-six, after going through the darkest time of my life, God cracked open my writing seed, and it has bloomed into a devotional blog and written talks for God's Kingdom. In His perfect timing, God unleashed the power of this light-seed so that my writing had purpose—for His glory. I ran from the fear, and I said yes to the opportunities that allowed His beautiful light to bloom. Now, God's light is shining through, and others are taking notice.

What are your dreams? What tugs at your heart? What did God plant in you? What is your light-seed? *We all have at least one. Maybe it is on this list—God is waiting for you to name it, to say it out loud, and to allow Him to bring it to life.*

- Adoption
- Art
- Counseling
- Foster Care
- Healing
- Ministry
- Missions
- Music
- Philanthropy/Giving
- Public Speaking
- Teaching

- Volunteering
- Worship
- Writing

Once we name our seeds, what do we do with them? Will we let them sit there in our souls, tugging at our heart strings as we simultaneously smother His light? I pray not! God provides these opportunities to crack them open, cultivate them, and grow them. God will support them so long as we take those opportunity gifts and do something with them. After all, the seeds were planted by Him for very specific purposes. This is how God asks us to "let our light shine."

In the movie "Evan Almighty," God (as played by Morgan Freeman) spoke to the wife of the main character. She doesn't realize it was God with whom she was conversing. He said something so profound that it stayed with me. "When people pray for courage, does God make them courageous? Or, does God provide **opportunities for them to be courageous**?" *I believe it is the latter. God will give us the opportunities to carry out the things He created us to do. I pray that we act on those opportunities and not let fear, pride, disbelief, selfishness, or distrust get in the way. "* ... with God all things are possible." *(Matthew 19:26)*

Psalm 97:11 continues, " ...**Joy-seeds** are planted in good heart-soil.**"** *Ah, joy! We all have joy-seeds too. According to Scripture, God planted them in our hearts. How do we unleash this joy? Heart-soil becomes good when our light-seeds are shining in perfect bloom. When our soul's seeds have matured and we have said* yes *to doing that which we were created to do, joy spills over. That is His promise.*

I often think about the other side of Heaven. I have no idea what it looks like, what I will feel when I get there, or all the questions that may be answered when I arrive. I do know this: I do not want to get there and find out I had a light-seed that I kept buried in fear's darkness. I do not want God to show me all I could have accomplished for Him and all I could have become had I said yes to that seed and the opportunities God gifted to crack it open. I want His light and joy to pour out of me. I want people to look at my one shot at a life of significance, to be drawn to that light and joy, and for them to say, "I want that."

I bet many of us want that. God's light is waiting for us. And, when it cracks open and we live in its full bloom, people will take notice …

So, here we are. God and I have spent three and a half years together on this book. It has been hard. There have been many ups and downs. The enemy has tried to thwart the progress on several occasions. But I have learned that God doesn't call us through the doors marked "easy." I have learned to depend on Him, to pray for His hand to be on me, and to say "yes" when He calls.

This book is not meant to convince others to stay in their troubled marriages. Those decisions are not for me to weigh in on when it comes to anyone else. Every marriage story has different details, ones that may change what God might ask of those facing those details. For me, the request was, "Don't leave yet."

I hope this book will reach those who are at rock bottom, those in their own ravines, and those with cracks zig-zagging all over their clay jars. This story isn't just about marriage. Cracks in our clay jars come from many sources. Whether you are a Christian or not, if you are a Jesus "Fan" or "Follower," or if you just picked up this book because you thought the cover was interesting, I have a message for you:

When your jar cracks (because it will) …
Jesus comes.
Take refuge in Him.
You will not shatter.
You will not be crushed.
God wants to make it good.
Let Him.
Trust Him.
Follow Him.
It's worth it.

COMPLICATED

I kept in touch with my "friend" from the support group for a short time after the ten weekly sessions ended. One evening, I sent her a quick email to check in and ask how she was doing.

How's it going?

Her reply was simple. It was perfect. It truly encompassed how my life with a recovering sex addict could be described.

It's complicated.

My husband and I have often thought that working through any other addiction would have been easier, at least as a married couple. Of course, we don't know that for sure because we haven't dealt with any other addiction. However, sex addiction clobbers the heart of a marriage. It clobbers its purpose. It clobbers its soul. Sex addiction forces its way into the intimate places where nothing and no one should be allowed to enter. No one except the Lord.

Alcohol. Drugs. Gambling. Tobacco. Exercise. Shopping. Eating. There are countless outlets for those with addictive behaviors to use to cope with their underlying dysfunction and pain. None affects a marriage like sex outside the marriage bed. It is not just a physical and emotional hit to the relationship. It is a spiritual one.

I am not here to wrap up this story with a nice red bow and package our marriage for presentation to you as perfect. It's not. Nor will it ever be. Even though Marc and I healed individually and as a couple, there are times when I find myself saddened by the intimacy crack in our marriage. There are times when we are alone and past emotions creep in, and I have to intentionally block them out. It's one of the prices Marc and I had to pay for what happened. Thankfully, it's not often.

I don't live in the past much. After all, I can't start the next chapter of my story if I keep re-reading the last one. However, as the chapters of our marriage story progress, and as God keeps pointing us in the right direction, we do find hope. We find peace. We find joy.

We have our disagreements and challenges, just like every other couple. And, at times, those arguments trigger a memory or a still unresolved issue in our marriage. But, we are two imperfect people who have learned to look up first and rely on a loving God to make the marriage better with each passing day. We have grown closer. We have learned how to be authentic and communicate well. We are still a team. However, now it's a team of three, with God in the coach's role. Others often ask us how we are doing. It's a challenging question with no right answer. I take that back. There is a right answer.

It's complicated.

But, it's good.

"No one lights a lamp and hides it in a clay jar or puts it under a bed. Instead, they put it on a stand, so that those who come in can see the light. (Luke 8:16, in the NIV)

ABOUT THE AUTHOR

Cortney Donelson holds a Master's Degree from Ithaca College in New York and professional certifications in human resources and the health sciences. However, she was compelled to pursue her dream of writing, speaking, and coaching after experiencing one of the greatest tragedies a marriage can face. Her book *Clay Jar, Cracked*, her devotional blog, "As a Clay Jar," and her involvement with the speaking ministry, icuTalks, Inc. are the products of her passion, faith, heart to encourage others, and God's provision.

A free eBook edition
is available with the
purchase of this book.

To claim your free eBook edition:

1. Download the Shelfie app.
2. Write your name in upper case in the box.
3. Use the Shelfie app to submit a photo.
4. Download your eBook to any device.

Shelfie

A free eBook edition is available
with the purchase of this print book.

CLEARLY PRINT YOUR NAME ABOVE IN UPPER CASE
Instructions to claim your free eBook edition:
1. Download the Shelfie app for Android or iOS
2. Write your name in **UPPER CASE** above
3. Use the Shelfie app to submit a photo
4. Download your eBook to any device

Print & Digital Together Forever.

Snap a photo   Free eBook   Read anywhere

The Morgan James Speakers Group